Training Fencing

This book belongs to ____________________

Club: ____________________

Coach: ____________________

Training Group:

Training Fencing

Barth/Barth

Meyer & Meyer Sport

Original title: Ich trainiere Fechten
Aachen: Meyer und Meyer, 2002
Translated by Susanne Evens, AAA Translation

British Library Cataloguing in Publication Data
A catalogue for this book is available from the British Library

Training Fencing
Dr. Berndt Barth / Katrin Barth
– Oxford: Meyer und Meyer, (UK) Ltd., 2003
ISBN 1-84126-096-7

Aachen, Adelaide, Auckland, Budapest, Graz, Johannesburg,
Miami, Olten (CH), Oxford, Singapore, Toronto
Member of the World
Sports Publishers' Association
www.w-s-p-a.org

Printed and bound by Finidr – s. r. o. Vimperk
ISBN 1-84126-096-7
E-Mail: verlag@m-m-sports.com
www.m-m-sports.com

Contents

CONTENTS

Hi, there! It's me, Foily!
Congratulations – you have learned the basics of fencing. Now it's time to start training, and I'm here to help.

Foily symbols you'll see in this book:

When this symbol appears, Foily has a helpful tip for you. You can read about mistakes to avoid or find useful advice.

This symbol marks exercises you can follow when you practice at home, outside of your regular coaching sessions.

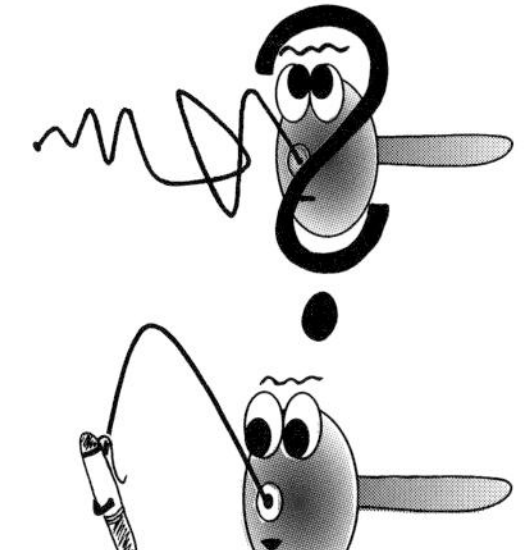

Here you'll find a puzzle or a question. The answers appear in Chapter 13.

Foily's pencil means it's time to fill in the blanks with your own information and ideas.

Date	*Competition*	*Place*	*Satisfied?*
February 3, 2003	*Club Championships*	*5th*	☺

1 Dear Fencer

This book is called *Training Fencing,* and for good reason. You're a fencer now; you're not a beginner anymore. You've spent many long hours in the fencing hall learning the basics of fencing.

The book *Learning Fencing* helped to introduce you to many important aspects of fencing. By now, you have had the chance to enter fencing competitions and use the skills you have learned.

How did you do?

In the table on page 8, enter the names and dates of your first tournaments. In the third column, record how you placed.

In the last column, enter one of these symbols to show how you feel about the result.

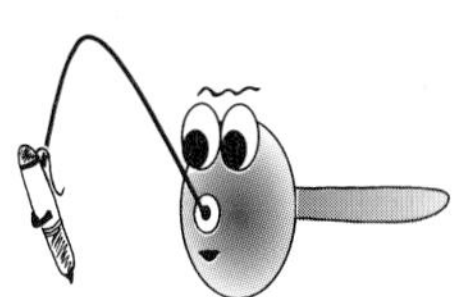

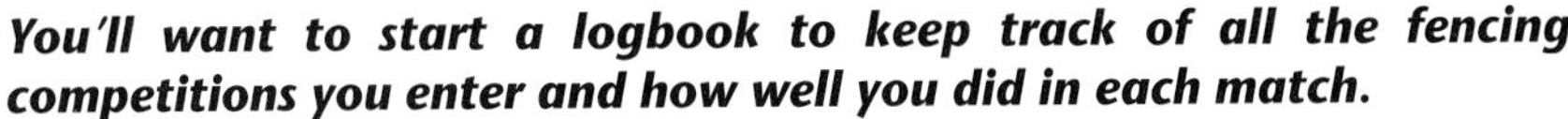

You'll want to start a logbook to keep track of all the fencing competitions you enter and how well you did in each match.

What comes next?

First, a little story:

Hiking in the mountains, a strong young man decided to climb to the top of a high peak. He cheerfully packed up food and water and set out in high spirits. Because he wasn't sure of the trail, he had some difficulty. He struggled up along one path, but when it faded to nothing he had to turn around and start all over.

The extra distance cost him a lot of effort. But every now and then, he was lucky enough to find a path that took him a little farther. After many such attempts, he reached the summit, where he found other hikers already enjoying the view. They told him that a good hiking trail led right to the top. He could have followed the trail instead of taking so many wrong turns.
Why hadn't he used a map or a guidebook, or at least asked someone who had hiked to the summit before?

The eager mountain climber in this story can help you as you start to train for fencing. Many athletes before you have trained for fencing and achieved good results. You don't have to start from scratch to figure out fencing and invent a training program. Instead, you can learn from the experiences of other fencers before you. That will make it much easier.

This little book, *Training Fencing,* can serve as a map, a guidebook to show you how you can climb the mountain of fencing without getting lost along the way. And of course you also have a fencing coach who can show you the right path.

You may find that experienced fencers, coaches, and authors of books about fencing have different opinions about movements or positions. That's normal. If something is not clear to you, ask questions and discover the reasons behind other people's different views.

But before you tuck this book under your pillow, fall asleep, and think you will wake up in the morning as a winner, we would like to say one more thing about the path to the summit:

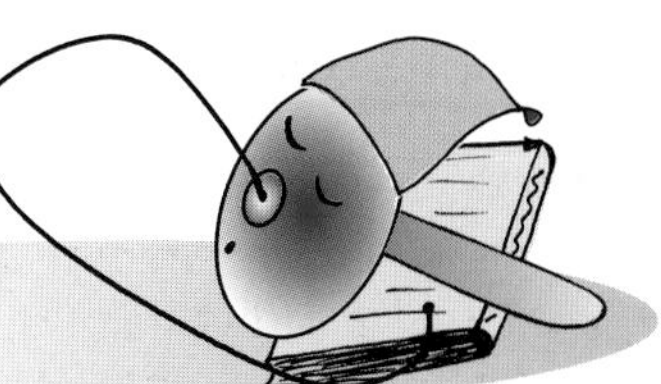

We want to give you advice and explain to you how to train properly. But only you can do the training. Whether you reach the summit or not is mostly up to you.

The explanations about training in this book apply just as much to girls as to boys. The same is true for coaches, who may be men or women. In our descriptions, we alternate between he and she, him and her, his and hers.

We hope you will have a lot of fun with this book. You will surely find plenty of interesting material here, which will help you travel the path to the summit quickly and safely. Good luck!

The authors and Foily.

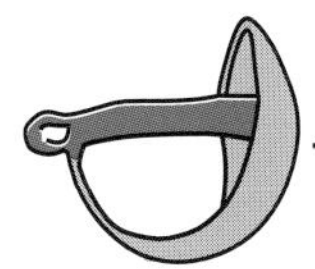

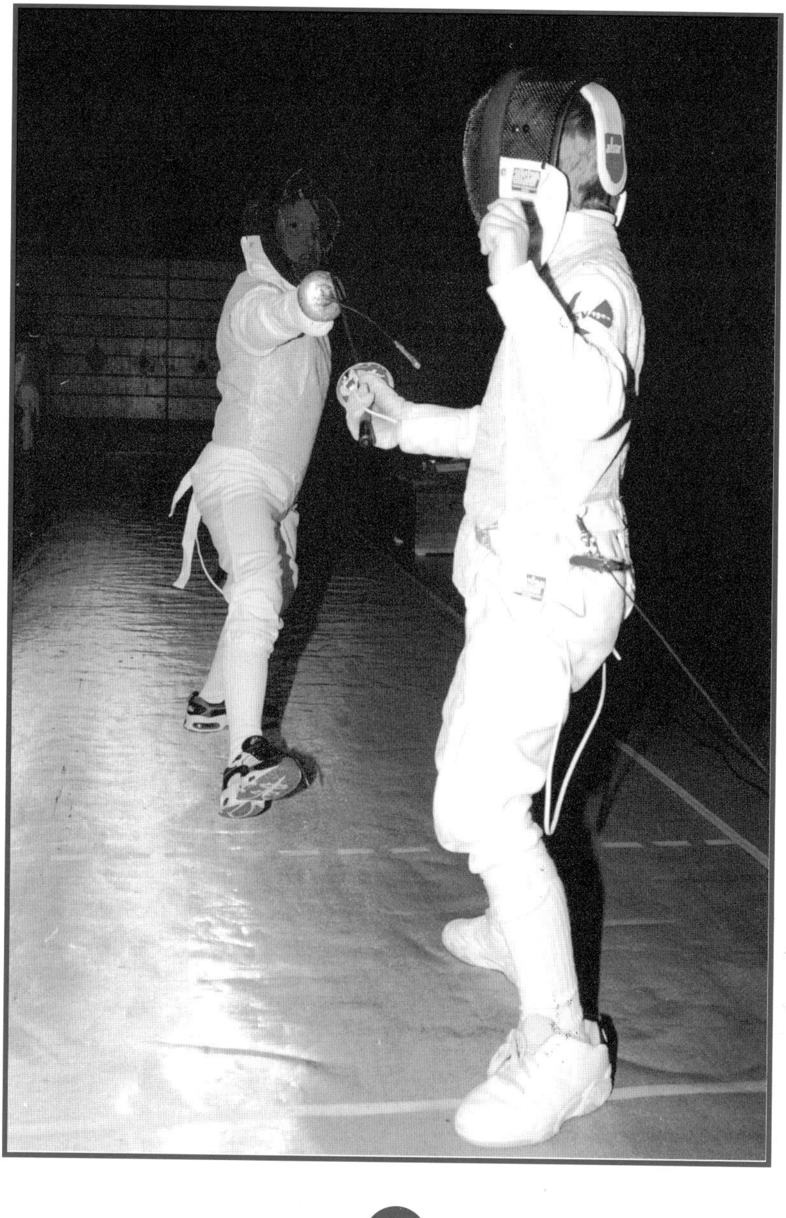

2 From Duel to Sport

The earliest drawings that have been found indicate that humans always did something like fencing. Their weapons were sticks, bamboo poles, and later also metal rods that they could use to strike and thrust. They fought like this when a person's body, life, or property was threatened. But there were also exhibitions that celebrated the art of combat. In those days, such contests were gruesome! Often the spectators waited eagerly to see one of the combatants fall to the ground, pierced through or even dead.

Starting in the 15th century, soldiers used firearms in war and other battles, largely replacing the less powerful fencing weapons.

Little by little, fencing developed into a pure sport. Fencers began to use lighter weapons that they could wield with greater skill and speed.

As time went on, Italian fencing masters brought order to the wild battles. They developed rules and established standard positions for the hand and blade. These are the basis for our present-day weapon positions. In Europe, fencing schools were founded and books were written about the sport of swordsmanship.

Primarily young men from rich families, nobles, and students turned to the sport of fencing to harden their bodies and prove their courage. They met in clubs or studied under famous fencing masters.

A young man who mastered the art of swordsmanship and proved his bravery and manhood in a duel won honor and high regard. Of course, even in those days a few progressive girls and women learned to fence. At that time, female fencers were unusual; today we take them for granted.

We found this drawing in a book about sports published in 1891. It shows young men practicing fencing. (From Des deutschen Knaben Turn-, Spiel- und Sportbuch, Bielefeld/Leipzig, 1891.)

Some young fellows enjoyed the rollicking life of students. They formed "associations" where they met to fight with fencing weapons. Usually these were duels about honor and tests of courage. Anyone who didn't want to participate in these wild and sometimes bloody fencing battles was ridiculed as a weakling.

A wound on the face, known as a cut, was considered a sign of manhood and the fencer was proud of the scar. These fights among students sometimes ended in death, and the universities finally stopped them by prohibiting the use of the epee in duels.

Fencing was revived later in Germany and citizens established fencing clubs. The German fencing association (the Deutscher Fechter-Bund, DFB) was founded in 1911.

Fencing in Germany

After World War II, German fencers at first went separate ways. The Deutscher Fechter-Bund was revived in West Germany, while the Deutsche Fecht-Verband (DFV) was formed in East Germany.

In both associations, it was soon recognized that peak athletic performance demanded many years of intensive training.

Special training centers were established, for example in Tauberbischofsheim and Bonn in West Germany, Leipzig and Potsdam in East Germany. Here the best fencers from each part of Germany could train together under the most successful coaches. Special schools also made it easier for young athletes to combine education and intensive training. Physicians specializing in sports medicine took care of the fencers, because only a healthy person can train properly.

Of course, the German fencers wanted to keep up with the top fencers around the world and succeed in international competitions. Sports scientists soon recognized that it was time to depart from classical fencing. Winning athletes could not continue fencing in the same way as fifty years ago. Experts in training methodology researched and developed training methods and ideas. For example, the Tauberbischofsheim training center introduced an innovative regimen with daily lessons, many competitions right from the start, and an environment that encouraged effort. The program also emphasized better education for the trainers and coaches.

The West German fencers won many international medals and always ranked among the most successful athletes. Although the East German fencers had a harder time and did not receive the same financial support, they too occasionally celebrated their place in an international final or even on the podium at world championships or the Olympics.

The German fencing teams were reunited in 1990. Though they sometimes struggle to reconcile the varied opinions and views of their coaches and researchers, they have laid out ambitious plans toward a common goal.

We look forward to a successful future. Maybe you will be among the fencers who win a medal in a world championship or at the Olympics.

Fencing Internationally

The international fencing federation, **the Fédération Internationale d'Escrime (F.I.E.)**, was founded in 1913.

There is also a European fencing confederation, **the European Fencing Confederation (EFC) or Confédération Européenne d'Escrime (CEE)**.

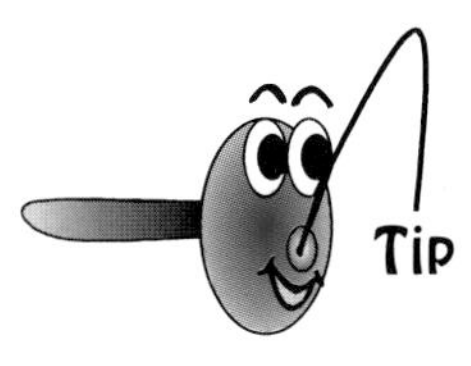

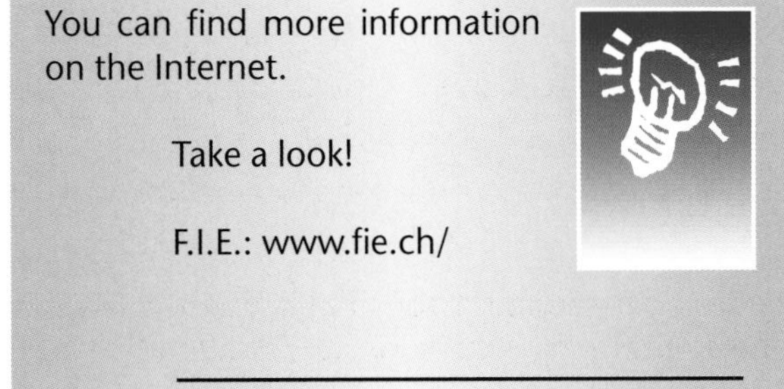

You can find more information on the Internet.
Take a look!
F.I.E.: www.fie.ch/

International Tournaments

World Championships are held every year for

Cadets: You must be younger than 17 years old on January 1 of the year in which the world championship is held.

Juniors: You must be younger than 20 years old on January 1 of the year in which the world championship is held.

Open: World championships are not held in Olympic years.

Seniors: Tournaments for fencers over 40 years old.

European Open and **Junior Championships** are held each year.

The F.I.E. rulebook was first adopted in June of 1914 by the International Congress in Paris. Since 1919, it is known as the *Règlement pour les Épreuves* (Rules for Competition).

............3 A Chat with an Olympic Gold Medalist and World Champion

Hello,
Sabine Bau!

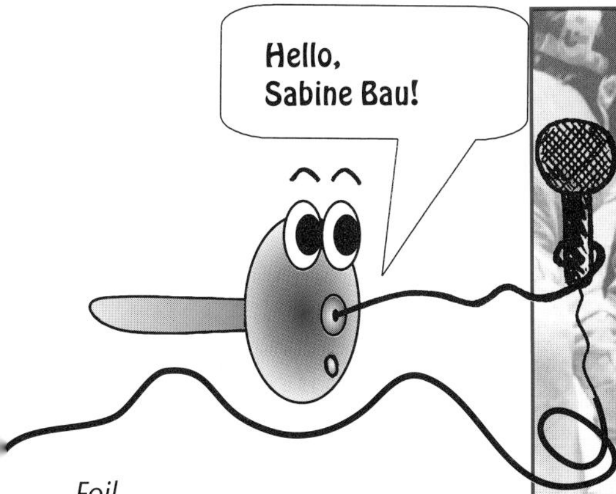

Foil
Born July 19, 1969,
in Würzburg, Germany
Olympic Gold Medalist and
World Champion
5 feet 10 inches tall, 146 pounds
Occupation: Physician

Sabine, you are a very successful fencer. Can you tell us your secret?

There's no secret. I just love to fence. I always wanted to improve and to win my bouts. I trained for those goals. And when there weren't any foil fencers left who were better than I was, I became the World Champion.

But of course, that didn't happen very fast. It took 20 years. I started learning to fence when I was nine years old, and I didn't win the world championship until 1998, when I was 29 years old. But I won my first individual medal long before that.

How does someone keep on training for so long?

Well, naturally I had many good results over the years that showed me I was on the right path. For example, as early as 1986 I came in second in the individual world championships, and in 1988 I was a member of the gold medal team and won an individual silver medal.

It's important to establish solid goals and to be able to celebrate every advance. Sometimes that can be a single touch scored, a successful action that you've just learned, or a better performance on a conditioning test. Then you know that your training has paid off.

And why did you choose fencing?

I started fencing without intending to make it a lifelong pursuit, but fencing is a very special sport. It's full of variety; you have to react quickly. Fencing is an elegant sport; it challenges and sharpens your thinking and it's very emotional. You're always going back and forth between being happy with yourself and annoyed with yourself. Training for fencing helped me not only to master my opponent, but also to master myself.

So training for fencing also helped you in other areas of your life?

Well, there were times when I really didn't feel like training or I was tired, and then I said to myself, "Sabine, you set out to do something, now do it!" And afterwards I was satisfied and proud of myself. So training taught me how to fight for goals I've set for myself. That helped me in school and in my medical studies.

With so much training, do you have any time for leisure or hobbies?

So far, fencing is my favorite leisure time activity and my best hobby. But school and my profession always came first. School and medical studies on the one hand, and fencing on the other, have complemented each other beautifully.

But of course I also spend time on other activities. I love to read, to travel, and to cook. I look forward to the time when my active career is over and I have time for other hobbies.

What advice do you have for young fencers?

Do what I did. To succeed as an athlete, you have to train hard, but you should also work hard in school and in preparation for your job, because you can't earn a living in Germany by fencing.

Thank you very much for talking with us, and we wish you all the best in the future.

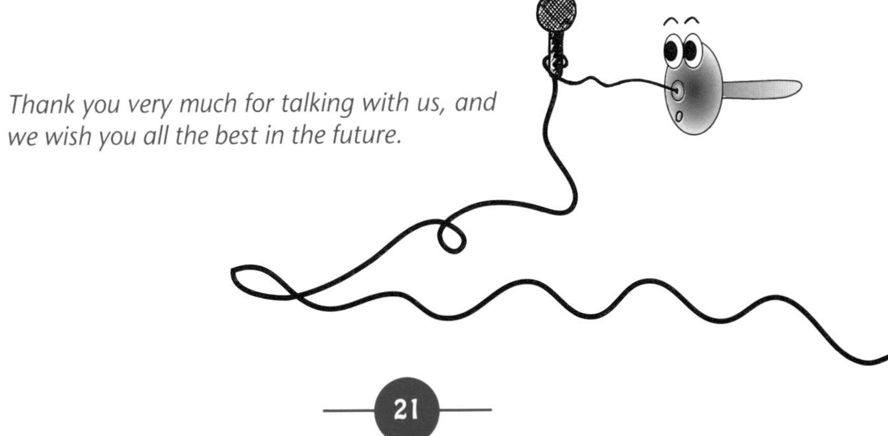

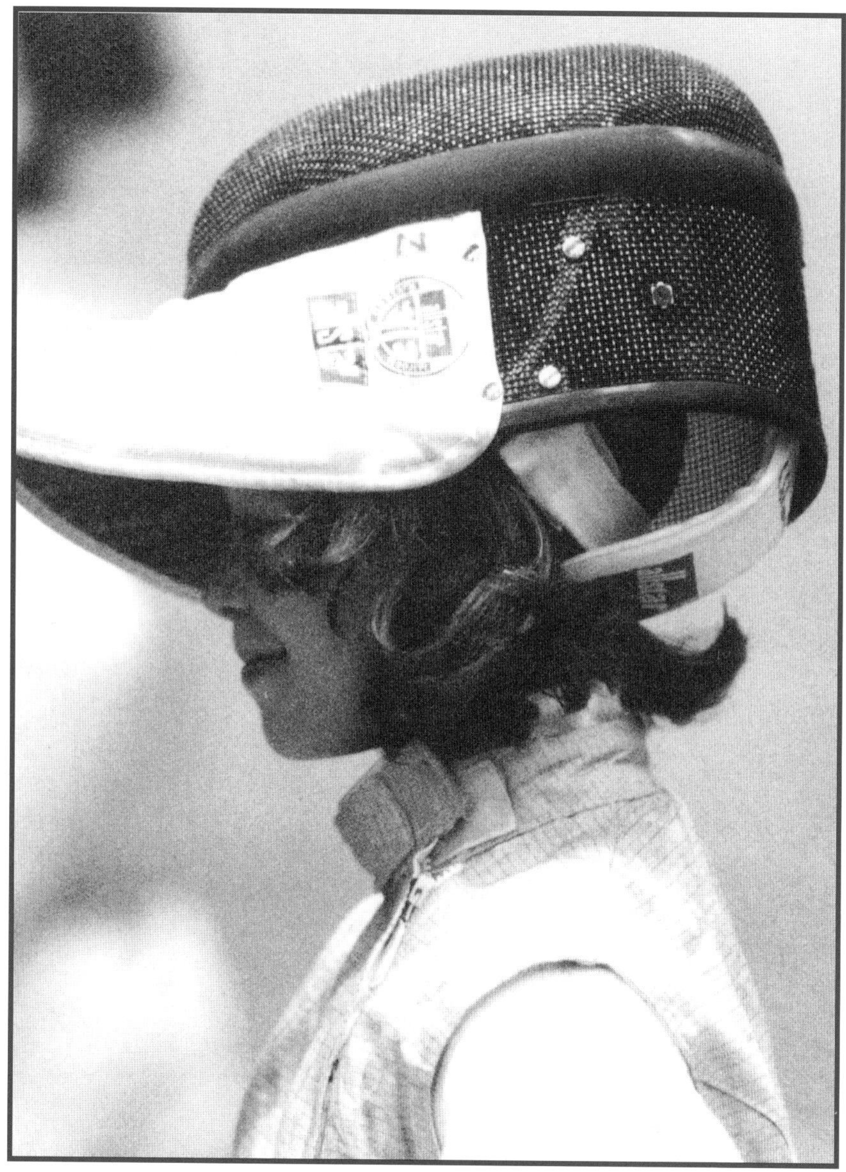

4 Training – The Path to Success

I want to achieve that kind of success!

Sabine Bau has given you some suggestions about the path to success. Maybe you have other role models as well – from your fencing club, from your national team, or from another country.

Write down the names of fencers that you admire and would like to emulate. You might try to get their autographs.

From Practice Sessions to Training Sessions

While you were practicing your fencing techniques, no doubt you often found that others could also fence well, maybe even better than you, and they would win the bout. But that's not so bad, because what others can do, you can do too.

We can anticipate your first question: "How should I train to become a good fencer, and maybe even a successful fencer?" We have written this book to help you answer that question.

The Path to the Summit of Fencing

This book is not intended to substitute for good coaching. But it will explain to you why your coach works with you to practice techniques and tactics, and why she says that you must improve your endurance, your strength, and your speed. You will learn why it is necessary to practice not only the fencing exercises, but other exercises as well, exercises that seem to have nothing at all to do with fencing.

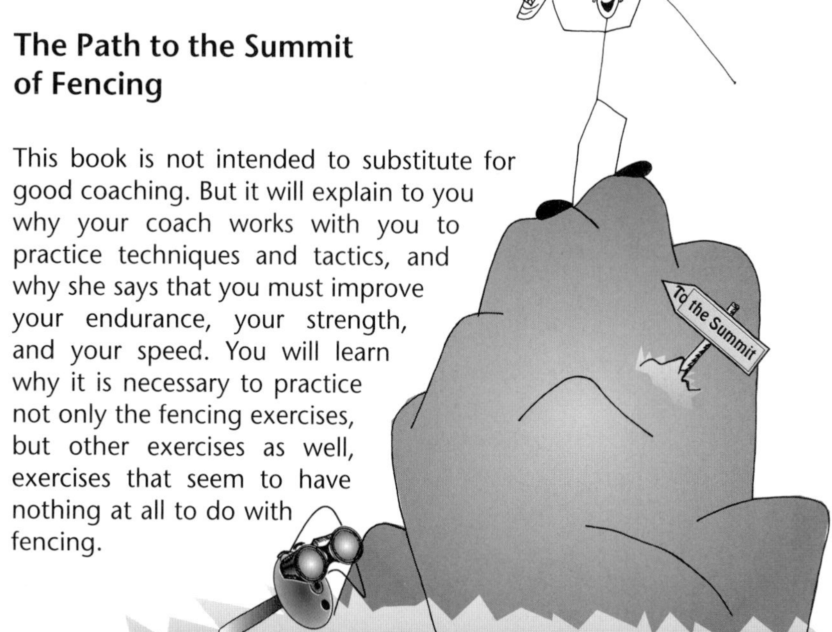

You will learn how important it is to warm up before your training sessions and to prepare yourself for competitions. You will find out why your muscles feel stiff sometimes and why you don't perform equally well every day.

You'll get advice about what you can do during practice sessions and outside the regular training sessions to improve your performance and to monitor and evaluate your own progress.

The best fencers can do this. After many years of training and competition, they know to a T whether they are in good form or not and how they must train in order to fence better.

They rely on the coach to be a good friend and advisor, but also a strict taskmaster when they are inclined to say, "That's hard for me to do. I'm calling it quits for today."

What Is Training for Fencing?

Training for fencing includes everything that you must actively and consciously do in order to become a better fencer.

- **Actively** means that you yourself must train. You won't become a better fencer by watching your coach jump or run or parry a thrust, or by sleeping with the fencing manual under your pillow at night. You must be an active participant in your training program.
- **Consciously** means that you understand what your coach is asking you to do, that you do it independently, and even that you sometimes think up and practice your own exercises.

An athlete's conscious training is the opposite of the sort of unconscious training that produces fast racehorses or greyhounds. They just do what their trainer tells them to do, without thinking about it – because they aren't capable of thinking in that way.

- Fencers train themselves.
- Animals are trained by an animal trainer.

Just as you can achieve in school only through active and conscious learning, so you'll do well in sports only through active and conscious training. You don't just do as you're told; you also understand why you are doing it. That's the key to success.

And because a fencer must train for many years to achieve excellence, it makes sense to learn right from the start what proper training means and how to train effectively. If you master these essential lessons, you will make greater progress than others in the same amount of training time, and in the end, you will be the winner.

What's more, training that way is a lot more fun.

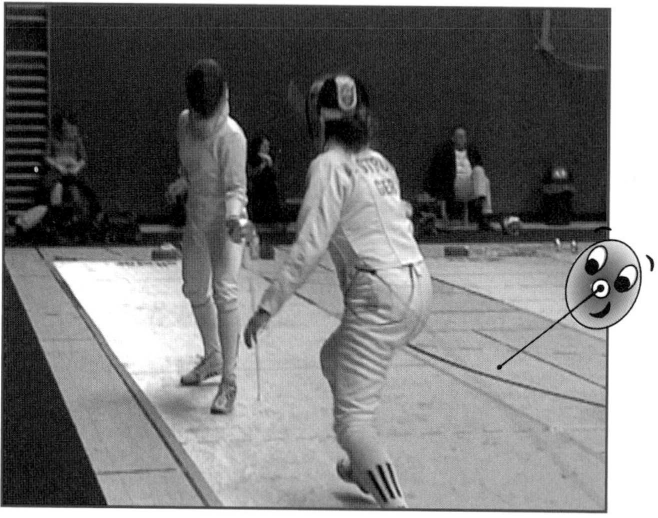

Train Properly – But How?

The prerequisite for conscious training is that you can answer these three questions:

What do I want to achieve?

This question addresses the goal of training.

You must know what you want to achieve. Active and conscious training requires clear goals. If you don't have a goal, your pleasure in training will soon flag, because you don't know why you're making the effort. Naturally, the most important goal of a fencer is to enjoy fencing. But you will only really enjoy fencing in the long run if you can win bouts against other fencers. You wouldn't enjoy losing all the time, would you?

It's only natural to start by setting a very grand goal: On television, you watch as a fencer who has won the Olympics stands atop the victory podium while the gold medal is placed around her neck. Everyone takes pictures of her and congratulates her. "I would like to achieve that too," you think to yourself.

And that's a good thing. But you should remember that your dream of victory is not yet a reality. A lot of sweat will flow before that, and you will have to swallow a lot of defeats along the way.

Even now, you often set goals for yourself. For example, you work to stand up from a lunge, feint, and score a valid touch. Maybe in the next match you want to finally score two points against Thomas, or to win a bout against Anna.

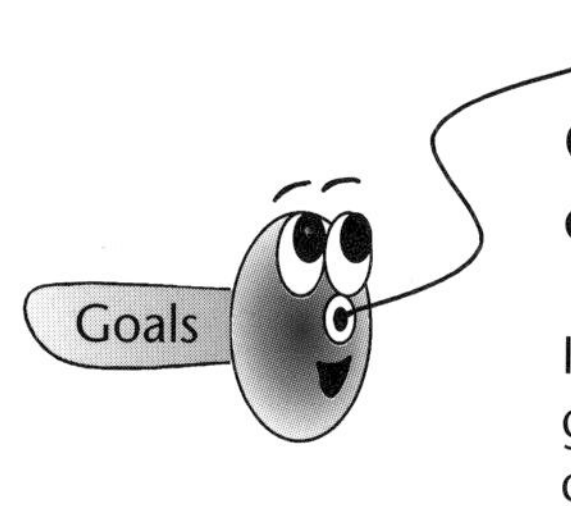

Goals are the driving force of the competitive athlete.

It's fun to achieve the goals you have set, and a goal that is just out of reach can spur you on to greater effort. But you shouldn't set impossible goals; a useful goal is realistic and achievable in the near future.

What's going on here?
Just a sec, Coach, I have to see what my next training goal is!

You may be asking why you can't just let your coach tell you what you can and should achieve.

Your coach will do that, of course. He also sets goals for training with his fencers and prepares training schedules that he follows when coaching you. In addition, coaching manuals offer training programs and other good ideas.

But you know your strengths and weaknesses better than anyone else. This puts you in the best position to set short-term goals for your progress as a fencer. Finally, when you set goals for yourself, you own them. As a result, you are much more likely to go all out to reach them. If you can tell your coach exactly what isn't working yet for you and what you want to practice more intensively in the near future, then he can get involved and help you in your training.

Naturally, coaches and athletes sometimes have differences of opinion. The goals you set for yourself may be at odds with those your coach has in mind for you. Try to understand the coach's point of view, and work with him. If he sets goals that you think are too high, take it as a sign that he has confidence in you. If you think his goals for you are too low, show by your actions that you are capable of more.

In the table on the next page, write down the goals you have set for yourself and the date. When you achieve a goal, put a check mark in the last column, with the date. You could also pencil in a target date for each goal.

When the table is full, draw up a new one and tuck it between the pages here, or glue it into the book. As another option, purchase a blank notebook that can serve as your "goal book" for months or even years to come.

What I want to achieve Date	Done! Date
Make it to the second round in the next tournament / October 22	(December 20) January 1 [check] ✔

Overall Goals and Partial Goals

An example:

Tom didn't do well in the last competition. But he knows the reason – his poor technique! He has set a training goal to improve his technique before the next competition, no matter what happens. That is his overall goal. Now, of course, he can't improve all his technique right away in the next training session. Therefore, he has set partial goals that will bring him to his overall goal.

You can see what this means:

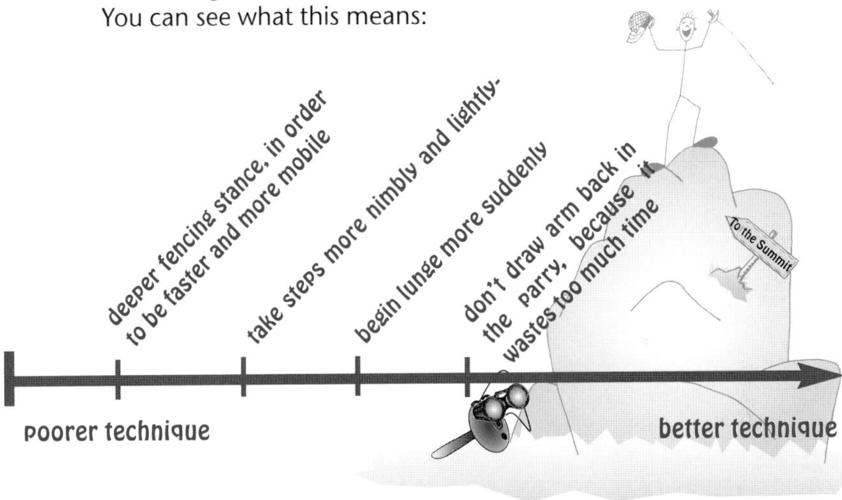
deeper fencing stance, in order to be faster and more mobile
take steps more nimbly and lightly.
begin lunge more suddenly
don't draw arm back in the parry, because it wastes too much time
To the Summit
poorer technique
better technique

Similarly, you can't improve a miserable lunge all at once. However, these partial goals can help you work toward a better lunge:

- Develop a fast lunge.
- Stand up more quickly.
- Hold arm steady.

You can set partial goals for all the techniques that are described in this book, and then you can celebrate when you reach them, even if everything might not yet go your way in a competition.

For conditioning, it's best to measure partial goals by using sprint times, endurance performance, or the number of repetitions of individual exercises.You can also set goals for mental abilities. But we will explain that in more detail later on.

Write down overall goals for yourself (as you did in the table) and then add the intermediate steps you will take to reach them.

Why do I want to train?

This question addresses the reason for training.

The reasons or motives for training are the "mental motor" that sets training in gear. They determine whether you go to practice or not, whether you fight for a win or let yourself give up at the slightest setback. When it's raining outside and you're bored, going to practice is easy. You'll meet your training buddies there and maybe have a good time playing around. But what happens when it's sunny and the swimming pool beckons, or your favorite show is on TV? Do you pack your gear bag just as quickly?

On the other hand, when you are absolutely determined to achieve an intermediate goal before the upcoming competition, and you know that the next training session is particularly important, then it's not quite so hard to make your decision.

Motivation – The Drive for Training

Another example:

> The coach says to Max: "Run 60 meters as fast as you can!" Max does his best and is happy with his time.
>
> Ollie runs beside him. The coach's stopwatch shows a faster time for Ollie. That bothers Max, although he had actually been quite satisfied with his own time. Max wants to race against Ollie again right away, because he doesn't want to accept this defeat.

Regardless of who won the second race, you can well imagine that Max ran faster than before. Spurred on by direct competition, he is motivated to try even harder.

If you care about what you're doing, it goes even better!

Naturally, a very important reason for making an effort in training is that you know why you must do the individual exercises and how they will help you to improve your performance.

Think for a minute about why you go to fencing practice and try hard during training. Decide whether a motive is very important, important, or less important to you. On the list on the next page, put an X in the proper column.

If you have other motives, add them in the extra spaces. You can come back to this list a year from now and fill it out again. Perhaps by then your motives will have changed.

I go to practice and work hard to do my best

because:

	very important motive	important motive	not very important
I want to fence as well as my role model.	☐	☐	☐
It's good for my health.	☐	☐	☐
I want to get stronger by training.	☐	☐	☐
I want to please my parents.	☐	☐	☐
I don't want to disappoint my coach.	☐	☐	☐
I want others to think well of me.	☐	☐	☐
I don't have anything else to do.	☐	☐	☐
I want to help my club win.	☐	☐	☐
It would be cool to see my name in the paper.	☐	☐	☐
It helps me learn to control myself.	☐	☐	☐
I want to make the national team some day.	☐	☐	☐
Fencing is a special sport.	☐	☐	☐
I can reach my goals only if I train diligently.	☐	☐	☐
______________________________	☐	☐	☐
______________________________	☐	☐	☐
______________________________	☐	☐	☐

How can I train so that I will reach my goals?

This question addresses the methods you use to improve your performance through training.

Practice without effort is not training!

In technical jargon, the effort involved in training is called load. Just as every fencer is different, so are her endurance and the training load she needs. When an athlete makes too little effort during training, she does not achieve any improvement in performance. On the other hand, working too hard can lead to fatigue and injuries.

Unfortunately, there isn't a table in which the fencer or the coach can look up how much the load should be and can be. The athlete must determine this for herself. Over time, she learns to "listen" to her own body and recognize when the load is sufficient.

If the training load is right, performance will improve because the body adjusts. The heart becomes larger and more powerful, and the muscles become thicker and stronger.

After a time of regular training, you will notice that exercises that used to make you huff and puff now don't take as much effort at all. Or if your legs once began to hurt in your legwork routine after five lunges, now you can add another five easily. Now it's time to increase the load. Your body will have to adjust again, and your performance will gradually improve.

For strength training, fencers do push-ups. To increase the load, the fencer should rest his legs on a stool.

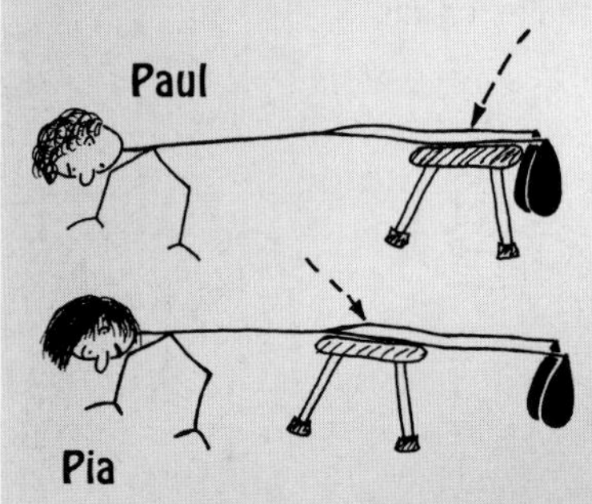

Pia has noticed that it's much easier if she rests her thighs on the stool. She laughs at Paul, who has to work much harder with his calves on the stool.

Who is "training smarter," Pia or Paul?

Training smarter is better than training harder

Many sports medicine researchers and physicians have investigated what training methods are most favorable for fencers to achieve the best athletic performance and keep the body healthy and fit. Simply training without thinking first usually will not bring the desired success. It can even be harmful.

Well-rounded Training

It's not enough to train just part of your body. Training must be balanced.

An example:

A quick lunge depends on certain specific muscles in your hips and legs. You can strengthen these by training with special exercises. Now, these could cause the opposing muscles (also called the antagonists) to become tighter. You could make the quick lunge, but it would always be too short. For this reason, a good training regimen includes stretching as well as to strength exercises.

Every trainer and coach develops a training plan to optimize his fencers' training. But of course you should not simply rely on your coach, but also think for yourself about what is good for you and helps improve your performance!

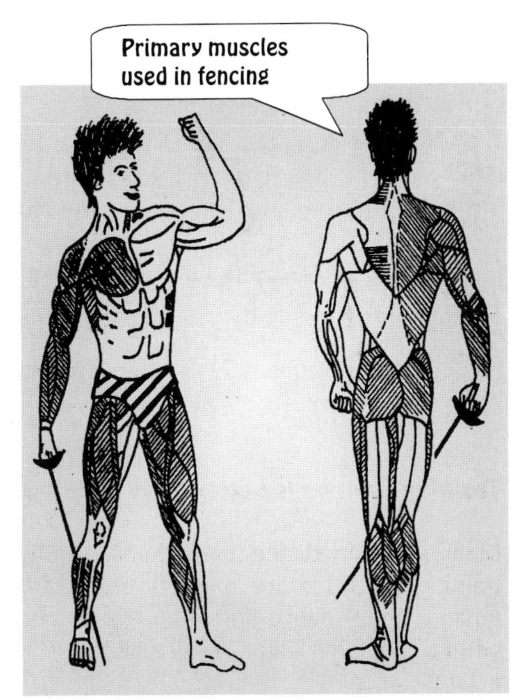

Here are some exercises that strengthen the fencing muscles and at the same time improve your sense of balance. Don't forget to do the corresponding stretches!

From a slight squat, lightly jump straight up, then jump left and right into the side step.

Lift your heels. Lift your toes.

You can do this exercise in a standing position, a half squat, or a full squat.

From a standing position into a squat.

You can do these exercises with your feet flat on the floor, on your toes, or on your heels.

To strengthen the arm muscles, you can work with small dumbbells or weights. Move the arms up and down, side to side, or bend them. You can also vary how much your knees are bent in this exercise.

If you don't use it, you lose it!

Surely you have noticed that if you haven't trained for a while, your performance suffers. In the first practices after a layoff, the exercises are harder to do and your skills are rusty. In that case, you must start with a lighter load than you were using in your last training sessions.

Regular training is better than sporadic training!

Do you recall our example of the summit you are trying to reach? Laziness and training lapses interrupt your progress. You lose ground. It's as if you have taken a few steps backward on the path to success. Of course, you won't always be able to train as diligently as you have planned. There are times when your schoolwork piles up, or your club can't reserve enough time in the fencing hall, or your coach doesn't have as much time for you.

Nevertheless, an athlete who is working toward a performance goal should train three or four times every week.

If you cannot train because you are ill or injured, of course you must take care of yourself until you are healthy. But if a vacation, a school trip, or another event keeps you from attending practice, you should try to stay in shape anyway.

Go jogging, do strength exercises in your room, and practice quick lunges or the various fencing positions. You will find special exercises on various pages in this book, and also in the companion volume, Learning Fencing. This will make it easier for you to resume training after a break.

What Makes a Good Fencer?

Suppose someone asks you, "What does it take to be a good fencer?" You can probably think of a few important qualities right away. A good fencer is quick, nimble, smart, clever, alert, brave… But the answer is more complicated than that.

In the diagram below, we have tried to show all the factors that influence a fencer's performance. The circles overlap, because the individual factors cannot be considered in isolation.

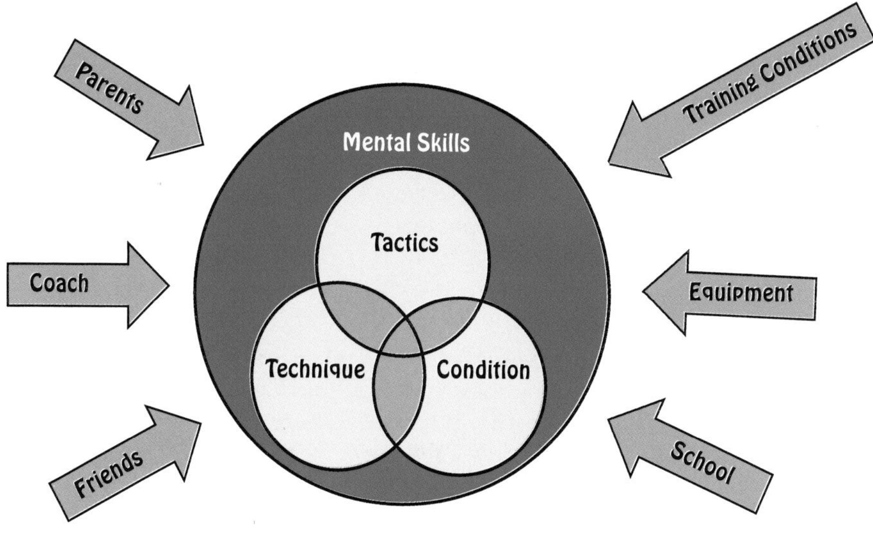

The circle of mental skills surrounds all the others, because it affects them all – like the software of a computer.

Tactics helps you to trick your opponent, to recognize her intentions or to draw her out and react properly to that.

Technique covers the specific movements used in fencing. These include the special fencing steps, the lunge, the way you hold your weapon, the positions and contacts. In fencing, it's important to concentrate on your opponent and the actions.

You must be able to execute the movements automatically, as if in your sleep. The weapon is your tool, an extension of your arm. You must be able to use it that way.

A fencer who moves quickly, has good endurance, and doesn't get out of breath readily is said to be in good condition. Condition is important in fencing; it allows you to make lightning-quick lunges and thrusts, not to get tired as soon in practice and in competition, and to be able to recover quickly after an effort.

Your psyche, or mental state, determines how confident or anxious you are, and whether a point against you or a defeat discourages you or spurs you on to fight harder.

You need good condition, for example, to become an excellent sprinter; you need clean technique to become a renowned juggler; you need sound tactics to become a successful chess player. But even all these together are not enough to make you a good fencer. If the psyche – your control system – fails, everything can fall apart, like a computer whose software crashes.

It's not easy to build up all of these components at the same time. To become a successful fencer, you must train each aspect, little by little.

Our diagram also shows arrows labeled parents, coach, friends, training conditions, equipment, and school. (You could add others.) These are all outside influences that affect a fencer's performance. It matters a great deal whether your parents support your training or oppose it, how well you get along with your coach, and whether you enjoy being with your training buddies.

When you have problems in school or stress at home, your head isn't clear. It also makes a difference whether you are training in pleasant surroundings or in a dingy, cold fencing hall with defective weapons.

Well done! I'm psyched!

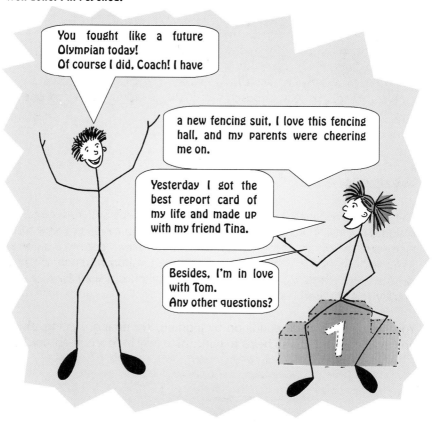

You fought like a future Olympian today!
Of course I did, Coach! I have
a new fencing suit, I love this fencing hall, and my parents were cheering me on.
Yesterday I got the best report card of my life and made up with my friend Tina.
Besides, I'm in love with Tom.
Any other questions?

5 Condition

Max doesn't feel well. He goes to the doctor and says, "Doctor, look at me – I'm getting all crooked! My right thigh is bigger than my left, my back hurts, my neck hurts, my hips hurt. And I'm having trouble with my feet, too. What should I do about it?"
"You should take up sports, young fellow!"
"But I do! I've been fencing for four years!"
"Show me what you do in fencing."
Max shows the doctor the advance, the retreat, and the lunge.
"And what about cross-training and conditioning?"
"What do you mean? All we do is fence."
"Well, then, I'm not surprised," says the doctor. "That's too one-sided."

What Is Meant by Conditioning

The term "condition" primarily describes physical abilities. Your condition includes how fit you are, how much endurance you have, and how much load you can tolerate. You can tell whether you are in good condition by noticing how soon you lose your breath during a short run, how long you can sustain an athletic effort without complaints from your legs, or how quickly you get tired.

You can develop good condition by jogging, swimming, skating, skiing, and even dancing. It also helps to participate fully in sports at school.

As a fencer, you need to be in good condition for quick leg movements, skillful blade control and endurance in long bouts.

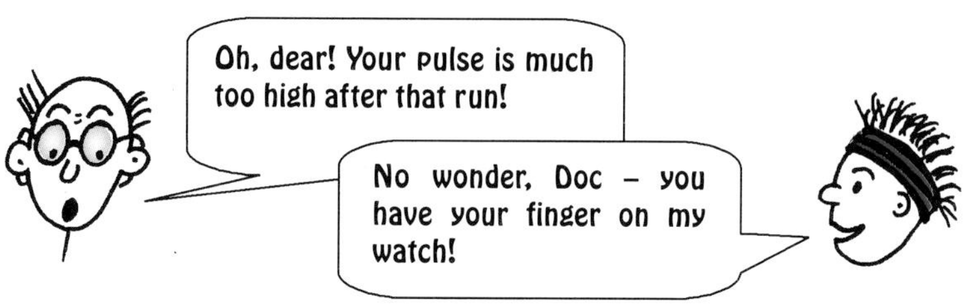

Oh, dear! Your pulse is much too high after that run!
No wonder, Doc – you have your finger on my watch!

Physical Abilities

The physical abilities that we need to stay in good general condition can be categorized as strength, endurance, and speed. Let's take a closer look at these elements of physical condition.

Strength

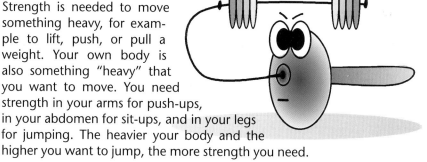

Strength is needed to move something heavy, for example to lift, push, or pull a weight. Your own body is also something "heavy" that you want to move. You need strength in your arms for push-ups, in your abdomen for sit-ups, and in your legs for jumping. The heavier your body and the higher you want to jump, the more strength you need.

Which sports require a lot of strength?

____

In fencing, you need strength in your legs for an explosive lunge and in your arm and fingers for secure and nimble control of the weapon.

For simple strength exercises, you really don't need any equipment. The weight of your own body is enough for exercises like pushups, sit-ups, deep knee bends or jumps from a squat. You'll find other exercises in this book.

Endurance

Endurance is the performance factor that allows you to sustain prolonged effort without getting tired. A person with good endurance is physically fit, recovers more quickly after training and competition, and can concentrate for longer periods.

Which sports require good endurance?

____

Fencers need good endurance, especially in strenuous tournaments. But fencing is not entirely an endurance sport; the brief interruptions throughout a bout mean that each individual effort only lasts a short time. Therefore, your training program includes relatively little endurance training. Its primary purpose is to keep your body healthy and strong.

You can build a good foundation of endurance by jogging regularly. You should run for at least 15 minutes without stopping, three or four times a week, at a uniform speed or varying your pace. Swimming, biking, and fast hiking also offer excellent endurance training.

Speed

The skill you need to execute a movement with optimum acceleration and swiftness is **movement speed**. You also need speed to react to a signal as quickly as possible. This is **reaction speed**.

Which sports require good reaction speed and movement speed?

The fencer must move his legs quickly to retreat or to change distance. Only a lightning-fast lunge takes the opponent by surprise with a thrust that is difficult to parry. For a fencer, the signals that trigger sudden bursts of speed are the actions of the opponent.

Once you know the technique of a movement and can carry it out, begin right away to execute it quickly. It's best to repeat the exercise a few times, but with full engagement and explosive force. If you always practice the lunge slowly and listlessly, you will not be able to execute it explosively in a bout.

And which sports require all three of the elements of good condition?

All Aspects of Condition Working Together

As you can imagine, the individual aspects of condition cannot be used and trained separately.

Speed Strength
If you want to execute a swift lunge, you need speed and strength to set your body weight in motion and sustain the movement.

Speed Endurance
Endurance influences whether your technique is still good even after prolonged legwork or your feet shuffle across the floor and your blade drags on the ground. For some fencers, the lunges get slower and slower after several repetitions and standing up from the lunge is harder and harder.

List the conditioning exercises you do outside of practice and check how often you do them!

Strength	daily	x per week	seldom
Endurance			
Speed			

W – S – S – S – C
(Warm up – Stretch – Strengthen – Stretch – Cool down)

Whether you are starting a training session, about to exercise at home, or competing in a tournament – the same rule always applies! It is important to prepare your body for the upcoming effort. After a day at school or a good night's sleep, your muscles are relatively cold and stiff. Your breathing and heart rate are also on "normal drive." Take time to prepare yourself fully for the training session and the competition.

These exercises don't just warm up your muscles and get your whole body moving; they also get your head ready for the effort to come. During these exercises, you shake off all your problems and worries. You free your mind and turn your attention to what you are about to do.

Warming Up

As the words tell you – you get yourself warm! Vigorous and varied exercises improve the blood supply to your muscles and get them ready to work. Signs that you are warmed up are looseness, mobility, a slight reddening of the skin and a light sweat. Warming up prevents injuries such as a pulled muscle.

Good warm-up exercises include anything that gets you moving: jogging, easy jumping jacks, aerobics, ball games or running races.

All your training sessions surely start with this. But even when you exercise at home, compete in a tournament, or simply arrive late for practice: Don't forget to warm up. A few laps around the hall, jumping jacks or gentle lunges are things you can do by yourself.

Stretching Your Muscles

The main way to improve mobility is to stretch your muscles. You can't just strengthen a single muscle; you must always consider the opposing muscle, the "antagonist." This is always the muscle on the other side of the limb. Otherwise, you'll end up "lopsided," like Max in the story at the start of this chapter.

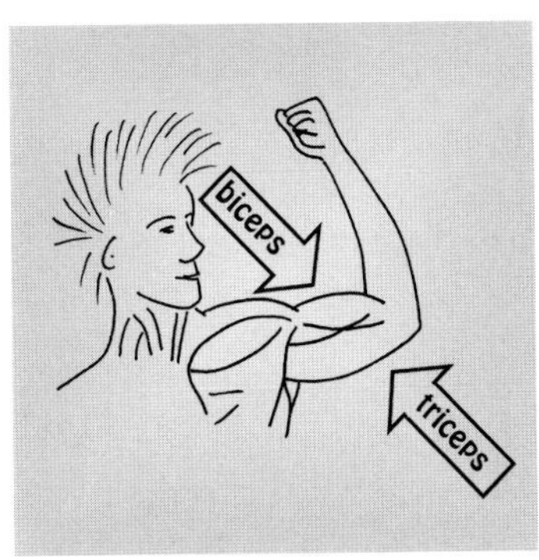

In the drawing, you can see the "muscle man" with his arm bent. The primary muscle responsible for bending the arm at the elbow is the "two-headed arm-bender." Anatomists call this the "Musculus biceps brachii," or **biceps** for short. This is the muscle that is tight when you "show your muscles" to someone. The muscle that extends the forearm is the three-headed muscle running along the back of the upper arm. This extensor muscle is called the **triceps**.

Now, what happens if the triceps contracts to extend the arm but the biceps, as antagonist, cannot stretch because it is too short? You would be unable to extend your arm, or could do so only slowly. Exactly the reverse would happen if the biceps tries to bend the arm and the triceps as antagonist restricts the movement.

That's why relaxation and stretching always go hand in hand with muscle training to build strength!

Feel your muscles! In the chapter on technique (Chapter 6), we will talk about "muscle sense." The same concept is used in muscle training.

Try the following exercise:

Exercises for home

Stand in front of a table with your arm bent so that the palm of one hand lies on the table. Now press as hard as you can against the tabletop. With the other hand, feel your muscles. The triceps is hard, because it is trying to extend the arm at the elbow. The biceps is soft, because it is relaxed and yielding. Next, place the palm of your hand under the tabletop and try to lift the table up. Now feel your muscles: The biceps is hard and the triceps is soft. That's the way it has to be.

Now try the same thing with the antagonist muscles at other joints, such as the knees and hips, or along your spine with your abdominal and back muscles. When you **stretch**, you lengthen the muscle group that has just been working.

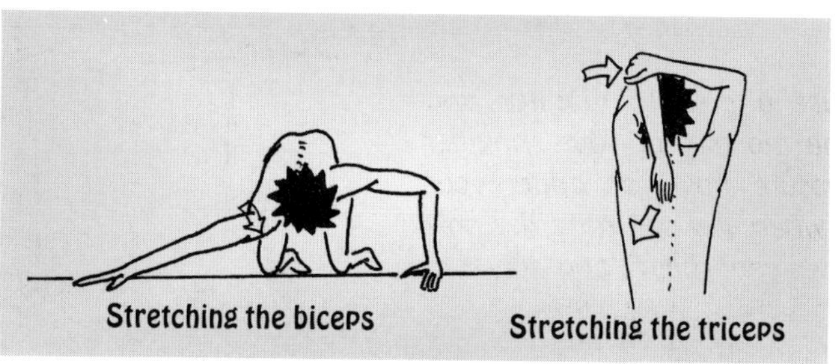

Stretching the biceps

Stretching the triceps

Relaxation

Although you have properly warmed up and stretched, after strenuous training your muscles are often hard and tight. Now it is time to stretch again, and then relax. Usually an athlete does this without conscious thought. You shake out your arms, legs and hands and move your limbs gently in all directions. Easy jogging or jumping also helps you loosen your muscles.

Test Your Flexibility

A fencer must be limber, for example to be able to make a wide and deep lunge. Here are a few exercises to test your flexibility!

You can improve the flexibility of your hip joints and the suppleness of your hip and upper thigh muscles by doing the splits. To keep track of your progress, measure the distance to the ground.

You can use a pole to monitor and improve the mobility of your shoulder joints. Measure how far apart your hands are when you can raise the pole easily above your head and lower it again without feeling any pain.

Here are a few stretching exercises. Can you feel your muscles? Have fun!

Stretch your muscles gently, without bouncing. You should feel a tug, but no pain.

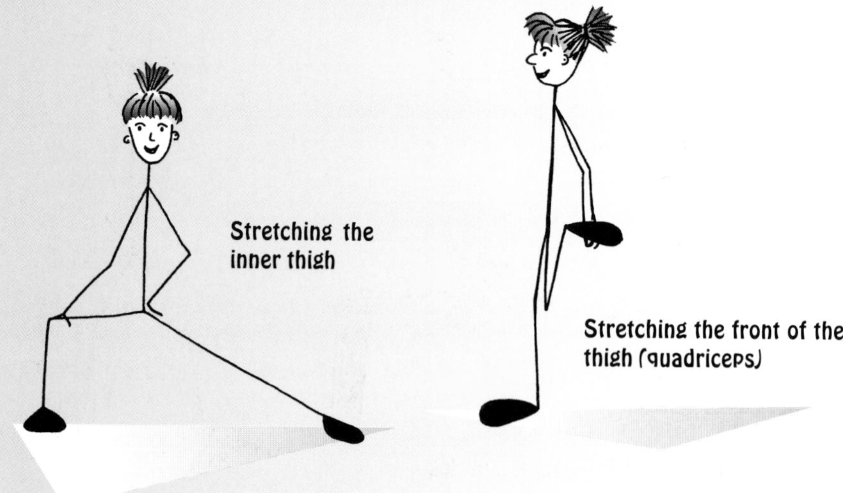

Stretching the inner thigh

Stretching the front of the thigh (quadriceps)

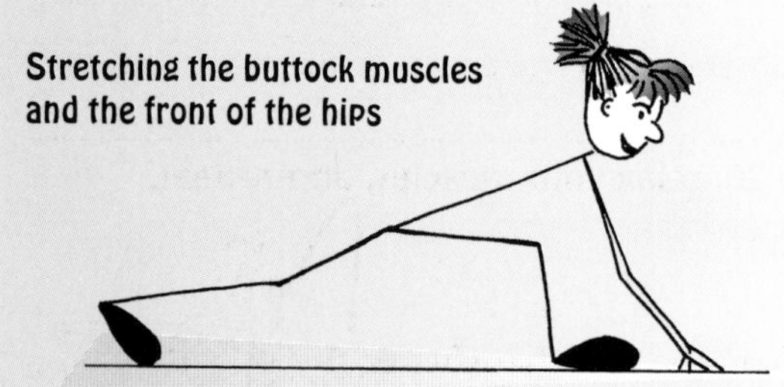

Stretching the buttock muscles and the front of the hips

Stretching the back of the thigh

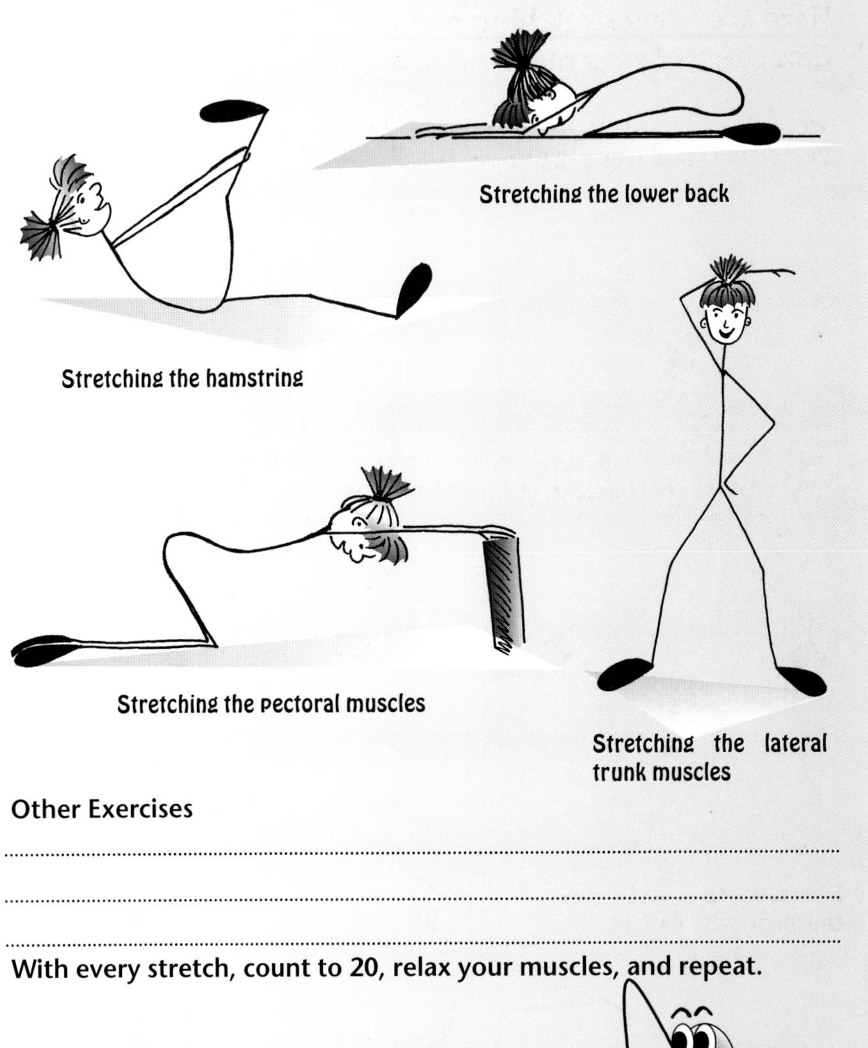

Stretching the lower back

Stretching the hamstring

Stretching the pectoral muscles

Stretching the lateral trunk muscles

Other Exercises

....

....

....

With every stretch, count to 20, relax your muscles, and repeat.

Tip

Keep in mind: The exercises should stretch the muscles. They should not hurt!

Strengthening Your Leg Power

We surely don't need to tell you here how important it is for fencers to have powerful leg muscles. On the next pages you will find some exercises that you can use to strengthen and monitor your leg power.

Vertical Jumps

Stand flat on your feet beside a wall or a post. Stretch your arms as high as you can above your head and mark this *reach* with a piece of tape or chalk. Now jump with both legs as vigorously as you can, straight up (maximum height). Mark your *jump height* at the highest point you can reach with your hand while you jump. (If you're doing this by yourself, hold a piece of chalk in your hand and mark the wall or post as you jump.

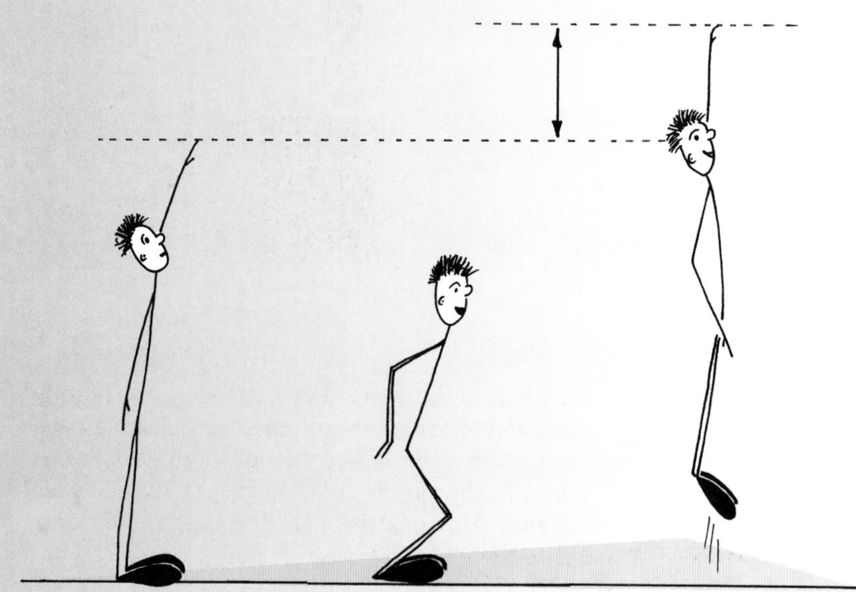

Of course, don't do this on the good wallpaper in your living room, or on your neighbor's white wall!) The difference between your *reach* and your *jump height* is your *jump differential.*

You can use this jump differential to have contests with your friends. Remember, the winner isn't the person who touches the highest, but the one who makes the biggest jump. Track your results, perhaps in a performance chart. As they improve, look for improvements in your training as well.

Deep High Jumps

The training stimulus is greater if you start on a bench or step, jump down, and spring up again as soon as you land.

Rest for about one minute after each jump. Don't forget to relax!

Stair Jumping

Stair jumping is a good exercise to develop the muscles of the ankle joint as well as the calf and thigh. Be sure to find a set of stairs where your hopping won't bother anyone.

Start facing the stairs, feet together, arms slightly bent at your sides. Now jump as quickly as you can up the stairs. Be careful not to trip! Your arms support the jump and help you keep your balance. This exercise calls for speed and lightness on your feet.

Variations:

- Jump up only a few steps and jog lightly back down. Keep adding a step or two as you go along.
- Jump on only one leg, left or right.
- Stand at a right angle to the stairs and jump up sideways.
- Jump two or more stairs at a time.

Two-legged Jumps

These jump exercises improve the explosive force of your leg and hip muscles and also strengthen your arms and shoulders.

Begin with your knees slightly bent. Swinging your arms vigorously, jump as high and far as you can. As soon as you land, take off in another jump. After six to ten repetitions, take a two-minute break and relax. You can do three to five sets of this exercise.

Variations:

Speed Hops:

Here you draw your knees up and forward as you jump. Try to touch your buttocks with your heels. The object is to jump high and fast.

Lunge Jumps

These jumps are particularly suitable for improving the muscles of your legs and hips, which you use to execute fast and long lunges.

From the step lunge (you can tell the difference between this and the lunge from the picture), jump straight up and land again in the step lunge. As soon as you land, jump again. Take care to jump as high as you can with each jump. Do this five to eight times; then repeat with the other leg forward. Rest for two minutes and repeat the exercise.

Variations:

Oh, Coach, I think I did too many jumps!

Scissors Jump

This is like the lunge jump except that you switch the position of your legs at the high point of each jump. Bring the back leg forward and extend the front leg back. The leg switch must take place very quickly and be completed before you land.

Monitoring Your Progress

It's fun to monitor your own physical development over time and the changes in your performance as you train. You can use tables and graphs to keep track.

height in cm

160
150
140
130
120

7 9 11 13 15 17

age in years

Sample Graph

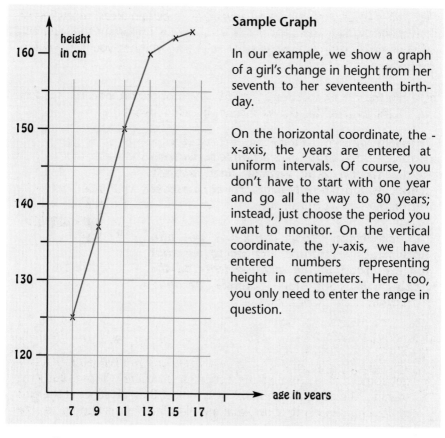

In our example, we show a graph of a girl's change in height from her seventh to her seventeenth birthday.

On the horizontal coordinate, the -x-axis, the years are entered at uniform intervals. Of course, you don't have to start with one year and go all the way to 80 years; instead, just choose the period you want to monitor. On the vertical coordinate, the y-axis, we have entered numbers representing height in centimeters. Here too, you only need to enter the range in question.

Naturally, you could choose shorter intervals; for example, you could enter a measurement every six months. Prepare a graph like this one for your height and a similar graph for your weight.

Training Logs

Fencers who train together tell each other about their results. Of course, the fencers who train regularly are likely to have better records, but keep in mind that other factors also influence the results. For example, an older fencer who has trained longer has an advantage over younger fencers. Also, taller fencers often have an advantage in certain areas, regardless of how diligently they train. For this reason, it's very important to keep track of your own progress. This is what tells you whether you are training properly.

You can track your progress in various areas of performance by making graphs like the one that shows changes in height over time.

To start your own training log, put together a notebook. It's easiest to use graph paper with the horizontal and vertical lines already drawn. Keep a separate graph for each aspect of training you want to track.

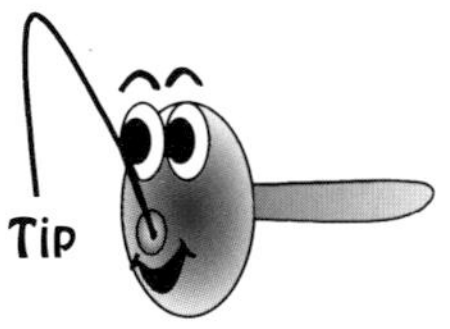

The coordinates along the x-axis can also mark weeks or months. Depending on what you are tracking, the measurements on the y-axis will vary, for example seconds, repetitions, meters, or inches.

Note:
Because you are getting older and growing, you will automatically get somewhat better and the performance curve will rise. But with training, the curve rises faster. Take a look at the guidelines at the end of this chapter, which show what a well-trained fencer should be able to do at different ages.

Exercises to Monitor

Here we describe exercises you can monitor to track your progress. Do them at home or during practice and record your results at regular intervals in a graph.

1. Speed: 30-meter sprint
From the race start position, start on command. Measure time in seconds. It helps to have someone else give the "Go!" command and measure your time with a stopwatch.

2. Leg speed: standing long jump
Because not all fencers are the same height, adjust by subtracting your height from the distance you jump. Start with your toes behind the start line. Jump with both legs. Measure from the start line to the rear of the marks you make when you land (the heel that is closest to the start line).

3. Arm strength: pushups
Do the pushups from your toes, as shown in the drawing. If you can't do a full pushup, start with your knees on the ground. Count the number of pushups you can do one after another without stopping.

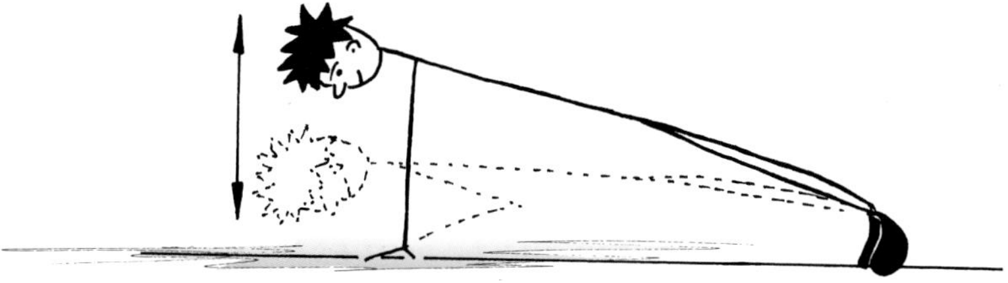

4. Basic endurance: 12-minute run
Measure how far you can run in 12 minutes. It's easiest to do this on a standard running track. Of course, you can run anywhere, but then you must go back and measure the distance.

5. Abdominal and back muscles: sit-ups
Lie on your back with your knees bent and your arms crossed on your chest. Sit up and lie down again. Count the number of sit-ups you can do one after another without stopping.

6. Reactions: reaction time
Your fencing club probably has devices for measuring your reaction time, because quick reactions are very important for fencing. Especially when measuring reaction time, the method significantly influences the result. Reaction times are shorter with a light signal than with a tone signal. The time for a simple reaction is shorter than for a selective reaction in which you must decide how to respond. Most of all, the distance to be covered in responding to the signal will determine the measured reaction time.

You might like to put together your own devices to test reaction time. Possible components include lights, noise-making devices, and timers.

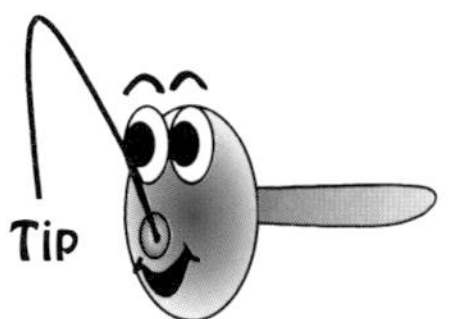

Of course, all these exercises can also be used as training exercises. To keep yourself from getting bored, simply vary the exercises.

Standards for Tracking Progress

The table below shows typical test results for a good fencer. You can compare your results with these. Keep in mind that these are only guidelines; your results will vary depending on how tall you are, how much you weigh, and how long you have been training.

Exercise	10/11 years	12/13 years	14/15 years
1. Sprint	6.0 – 6.5 s	5.8 – 6.4 s	5.7 – 5.3 s
2. Long Jump			
(difference)	10 – 15 cm (4 – 6 inches)	15 – 20 cm (6 – 8 inches)	20 – 30 cm (8 – 12 inches)
(absolute)	120 – 150 cm (47 – 59 inches)	150 – 170 cm (59 – 66 inches)	170 – 190 cm (66 – 74 inches)
3. Push-ups	8 – 10	10 – 15	15 – 20
4. Run	1700 – 2000 m (1 – 11/4 miles)	1900 – 2200 m (1.2 – 1.4 miles)	2100 – 2400 m (1.3 – 1.5 miles)
5. Sit-ups	8 – 12	12 – 15	15 – 20
6. Reaction time**	* Because the tests and therefore the reaction times are very different from one club to another, ask your coach to tell you what would be a good reaction time for your age group for the specific test you take.		

6 TECHNIQUE

Have you ever tried juggling with five pins or balls? Some artists juggle flaming torches or sharp knives, balancing with them while they ride a bicycle. Even the best juggling artists certainly didn't master this trick while they were in their cradles. When they began to learn, no doubt the objects they tried to juggle tumbled wildly about and fell to the ground. A person needs to practice such skills long and hard before mastering them completely.

What in the world?

Help, Coach,
I can't remember
how the retreat
goes!

A fencer must work just as hard to master the techniques of fencing. A good fencer must be able to concentrate on her opponent during a bout, attack at lightning speed, score a touch and defend herself against her opponent's attacks. She doesn't have time to stop and think. Imagine if you had to remind yourself of each individual sequence!

For example: *"Extend arm – un-weight foot – lift forward – kick leg – extend – hit – parry."*

The weapon is like a fencer's tool, and he must know how to wield it perfectly. To do this, he must master the individual techniques.

Another saying:
A fencer is an artist with the weapon!

Technique in Fencing

Technique in fencing means all the specific movements that are used in fencing and that are permitted by the official rules of the sport. These include the advance, the retreat, and the lunge, the thrust and the cut, the positions and changes of position, contact and disengagement, and many more. You have already learned the most important techniques in your early years as a fencer, and you will add more as you continue to train.

Technique in fencing is executed so swiftly, precisely, and reliably that the observer can hardly follow the sequence. Only the outcome tells whether the technique was right or wrong, whether the fencer has scored a touch or properly defended. It's like our juggler. He can no longer follow every grip and every individual object. The technique must be practiced until it works perfectly. If a ball or a pin drops, the juggler has made a mistake.

Find twelve special technical terms used in fencing!

KAONGDFUCONTACTLENGFEINTLOEBNKKGAJJDITTMER
KPUWMVJUMPOSPRULEFVPARRYSLPQMOPRIORITYFJOS
FLECHESHBIRRETREATAKLELUNGEWUOLQWDAFBSER
NMVACUSHJAFGABEATMNASSIOADVANCEDKLCCBOHA
TWBXKABUNOSLIOCTAVELOUVSTOATHRUSTGBAJOHRB

Training Technique

When you learn a new technique, you usually start with a description and demonstration by your coach. She explains the sequence, tells you what to pay special attention to, and warns you about mistakes to avoid.

Now it's your turn to practice the new technique. Naturally, it's a lot of fun to discover and explore a new technique. At first, you usually go through the movements very slowly and imprecisely, just watching to see whether your arms and legs are doing everything correctly. Maybe you have caught yourself repeating the sequence under your breath, as if talking to yourself. But that's normal; our juggler does the same thing.

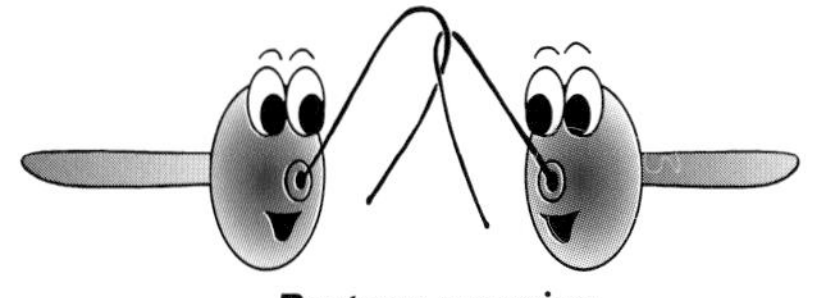

Partner exercise

Help each other! One athlete executes the movement and the other observes him carefully, telling him what he's doing right or what needs work.

Your coach will let you practice by yourself and give you tips now and then. You can see progress quickly. Your movements become steadier and steadier, faster and faster. As your coach observes your improvement, his praise motivates you to keep practicing and to become even faster and more precise.

But after a while, all that practicing begins to get boring. The novelty has worn off, and you no longer feel that you are really getting any better. You think, hey, you're doing well enough with this new technique, why should you keep on practicing?

Now the time comes when you may not be at all interested in practicing. But if you stop now, you'll forget what you've already learned, and all your hard work so far was in vain!

So think of your goals, and conquer your own lack of willpower!

After the initial stage of rapid progress come many other days of training when you have the feeling that nothing at all is happening. You can count on this. On the long road to perfect technique, there are always stages of rapid progress and stages of laborious struggle.

So when you think it won't ever get better – this is your limit of performance, and further practice is useless – keep plugging along, and you will find that it does get better after all.

When you think that your progress has ground to a halt, we would like to offer you this word of comfort. On this apparent plateau, your body is preparing itself for the next stage of development. It is, so to speak, reprogramming itself for the next advance. That sometimes happens almost as if overnight. So don't let yourself be discouraged by an apparent standstill. These are necessary transition stages.

Here the watchword is: Keep going!

Your coach knows this and will keep you diligently practicing and practicing.

Trust our advice:
Patient and persistant practice will win the day!

The Path to Improved Performance

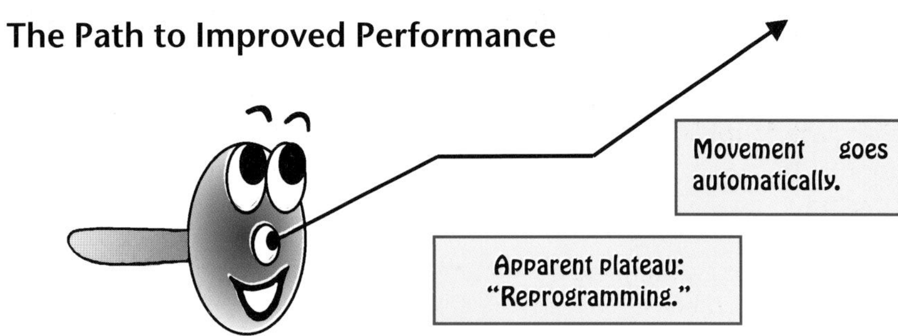

Movement goes automatically.
Apparent plateau: "Reprogramming."
The movements for the new technique are controlled very consciously.
You need to concentrate on every step of the sequence and follow the sequence with your eyes.

An example of learning a skill:

Do you know this little puzzle?
"This–is–the–house–of–Mister–Mouse."
The challenge is to draw the house in one stroke, without lifting your pencil from the paper. The drawing at right shows one way to solve the puzzle.

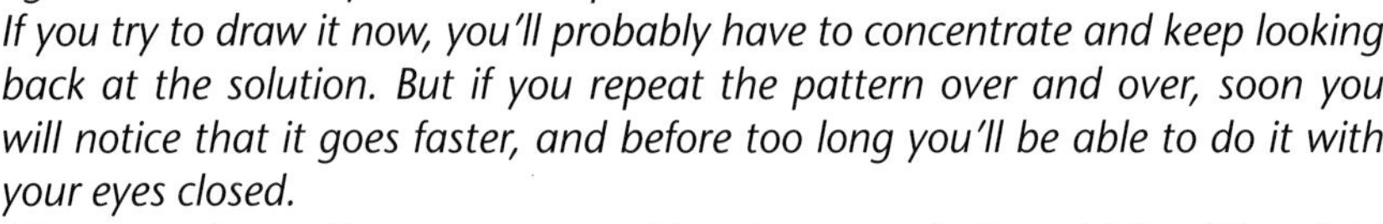

If you try to draw it now, you'll probably have to concentrate and keep looking back at the solution. But if you repeat the pattern over and over, soon you will notice that it goes faster, and before too long you'll be able to do it with your eyes closed.
After enough practice, someone could wake you up in the middle of the night and you would be able to draw Mister Mouse's house perfectly without even thinking about it.

Learning this little trick goes relatively quickly. To learn other skills, you must spend many, many hours in training, maybe even years. Remember the juggler?

Top Fencer with Individual Style

Because fencing technique is not a mathematical or chemical formula, naturally there can also be various approaches and slight variations among athletes and coaches.

In the course of his fencing career, every fencer develops idiosyncrasies or a style that he prefers.

Watch experienced fencers during a tournament. You'll see that their technique isn't always as "pretty" as you learn in practice. But even the older, successful fencers know how important it is to master good technique and always practice it in their training sessions.

Muscle Sense

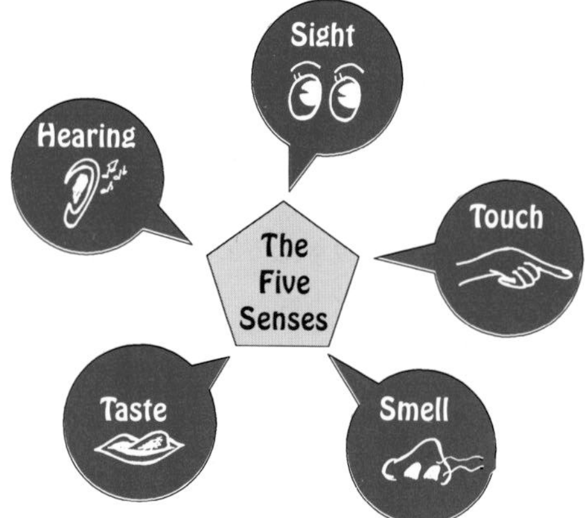

Parents and teachers often speak of the *five senses* that you should use when you're learning about something new. They tell you to listen carefully, look closely, touch the surface, smell the object, and find out what it tastes like.

Surely you have also noticed that all the senses don't always work at the same time and with equal power. Many people even speak of a sixth sense. By that they mean something like a feeling or a premonition.

Fencers, too, use something like a sixth sense for an awareness of their muscles and movements. We call this simply "**muscle sense.**" This is very important for learning and mastering techniques in fencing.

Proper fencing is fast. You don't have time to look to see where your weapon is and whether it's in the right position. You have to "feel" this. And this "feeling" or "muscle sense" is developed in training and by diligent practice.

Which Senses Are Important for Fencing?

You may be asking yourself: Does this mean we don't use our other senses in fencing? Of course you do. Not all of them, but some of them. The sense of taste is obviously not used in fencing, and the sense of smell is involved only if your fencing suit or your socks need washing. Obviously, the sense of sight is essential for fencing. But you also need the sense of hearing: You hear when the blades touch each other and detect the rhythm of the leg movements. The inner ear is also the center of balance. You need this sense to keep from falling down when you take fast steps or make a lunge.

Exercises for home

Stand in front of a mirror with your weapon and assume the sixte position (later also other positions).

Check yourself:

- *The guard is at a height between your chest and hips.*
- *The forearm is barely visible.*
- *The tip of the blade is to the outside next to your head.*
- *The inner target is unprotected; the outer target is protected.*
- *If the opponent thrusts outside the blade, he canít touch you.*

Repeat this a few times:

- *Fencing position – sixte – check yourself.*
- *En garde – fencing position – sixte – check yourself.*
- *Fencing position – move the weapon into various positions, up, down, inside, outside – sixte – check yourself.*

How did it go? Is your sixte position always right? Then repeat the exercises with your eyes closed.

Like this: Fencing position – close your eyes – sixte – open your eyes – check yourself.

Can you tell even with your eyes closed whether you assume the sixte position correctly in these exercises? Can you sense it with your muscles? Naturally, it's much easier to sense the positions with your eyes closed if you have practiced them for a long time. Next time, try it with your eyes closed right from the start.

Test how well you can keep your balance! Stand in the fencing position on the beam of an overturned balance apparatus and then execute fencing steps and the lunge.

Tips for Technique Training

- Listen and watch closely when techniques are explained and demonstrated!
- Visualize the technique. Close your eyes and concentrate on the sequence and the movement. Repeat this step a few times.
- Practice the technique over and over again. After every repetition, check yourself or have others tell you whether anything needs to be improved.
- In a quiet moment, look carefully at the drawings and descriptions and compare them with your own movements. It can be helpful to describe, explain, and demonstrate the techniques to someone else.
- Practice with various training partners, not just your favorite partner. Each fencer has his own style and you must be able to adjust your technique accordingly.
- Observe and help each other!

How many repetitions must a fencer go through before the technique works perfectly? This varies, just as learning in school varies. But every fencer must practice a lot. At the end, the technique should be executed quickly, precisely, and without conscious control, that is, *automatically*.

The many repetitions "program" the sequences into your brain and store them there. It's almost as if you are loading a computer program that you can call up later.

Consider this: If you don't make an effort in training, if you always repeat the exercises slowly and incorrectly, your brain stores the slow and incorrect sequences. Later you won't be able to do any better, because the wrong movements have become automatic.

Monitor – Evaluate – Improve

Do you recall the tips for technique training and the exercises in front of the mirror? Don't let incorrect movements become automatic!

That's why it's so important to monitor the development of a new technique, recognize your mistakes, and practice executing the movement faster and more precisely as you go along. How quickly you master a new technique depends on your goals and on your *motivation*. Do you remember?

Max, a novice fencer, is learning the lunge. He has paid attention and now he wants to follow everything the coach has told him. He works very hard the first few times he practices the lunge. The coach watches him and says,
"Way to go, Max! You're doing a good job!" Max is pleased and continues to work.
A few training sessions later, the coach watches Max as he practices his lunge again. This time, he says,
"That still needs some work, Max! Your lunge is too slow and you're standing up too straight!"
Max is upset. He is doing the lunge just exactly the way he did a few days ago. The coach praised him then, and now he's scolding him!

You have probably figured out that the coach in this story hasn't made a mistake. He has simply adjusted his evaluation to the situation and the possibilities. Max certainly wasn't doing the lunge perfectly the first few times he practiced it, but it was quite good for a first attempt. Later, however, after many repetitions, the coach expects to see an improvement. Max should have reached his next intermediate goal.

Monitoring by the Coach

On the path to rapid and precise technique, you will reach many partial goals. Every little mistake is observed and corrected. Evaluation by your coach is best, because she knows fencing and has mastered the technique very well. That's why the coach's lessons are so important in fencing.

But the coach can't always teach everyone at the same time, so you spend most of your training sessions working on your own. You monitor your own fencing and tell yourself whether you are doing well or badly. A fencer must be able to do that!

Sally was chatting with her friends during the practice session. The coach keeps her after practice for ten minutes of extra work with him. Is that an appropriate penalty?

Aids for Self-Evaluation

- First of all, you should have a very precise understanding of the new technique. You can get this by looking closely at the drawings and watching your coach as he demonstrates.
- Compare the proper execution with your own and identify any deviations. These are the errors that you want to correct. To help you, this book also shows drawings of errors – exaggerated images of the wrong way to do things. Take note of the mistakes your coach points out in your lessons.
- Set yourself goals for practice. Praise yourself when things go well, and scold yourself if you keep making the same mistakes.

It's best when your training partners take practice just as seriously as you do. Then you can observe each other in the partner exercises, evaluate each other, and give each other useful advice.

In many training groups, the fencers teach each other. They take turns being the student and the coach or fencing master. This is not only fun, but also an excellent way to make good progress.

Training Aids to Use at Home

If you like, you can make yourself some simple training aids to use at home.

Note: Be sure to construct the training aids in such a way that you can use them safely and will not injure yourself. When you train with practice dummies that hold weapons, wear a mask. Tell other family members what you are doing, and take care that nobody is injured (for example, by suddenly opening a door).

Target
Target with target area outlined
Target with a weapon arm
Target dummy: Here you can practice thrusts on the entire body.
Pendulum ball: Practice various ways of disengaging to evade the suspended ball.

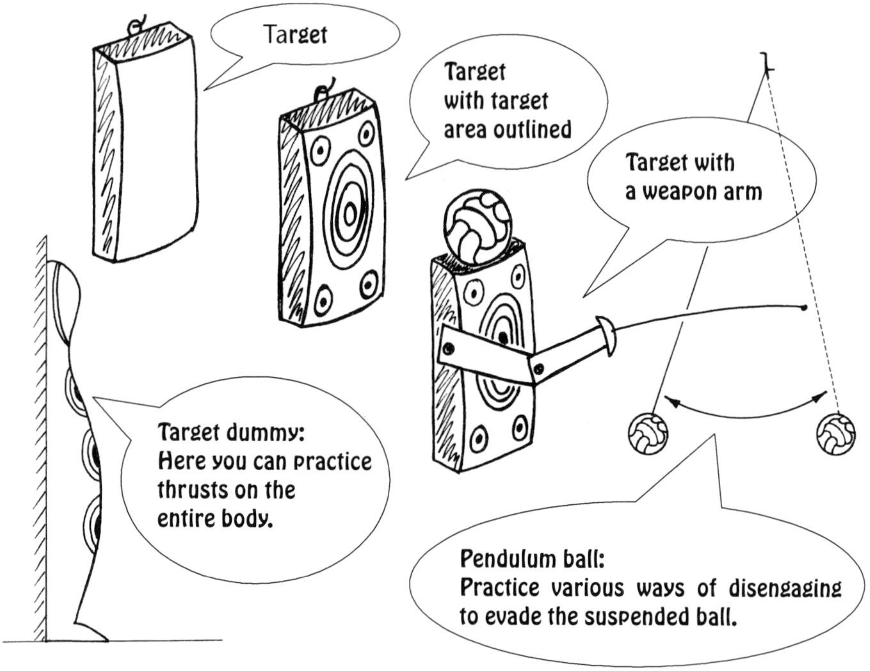

7 Tactics

Do You Know What Tactics Are?

Of course you do, because you use tactics even in your everyday life. It's just that you don't use this word to describe your behavior, and you use tactics without thinking about them.

Do you recognize this scenario?

> Max has received a poor report card and must show it to his mother. But he doesn't show it to her right away.
>
> First he cleans his room, takes out the trash, and helps his mother set the table. Casually, he mentions that he hasn't been doing very well in school. As if by coincidence, he brings out the poor report card, along with a pen for his mother's signature.
>
> Luckily, she doesn't scold him too badly!

So, does this little story sound familiar? It's normal, after all, when you want things to go well, to look for a favorable setting, or wait for the right moment, or prepare the ground before you ask for a raise in your allowance or a new CD. You are simply using good tactics.

Strategy is choosing the path that leads to success!

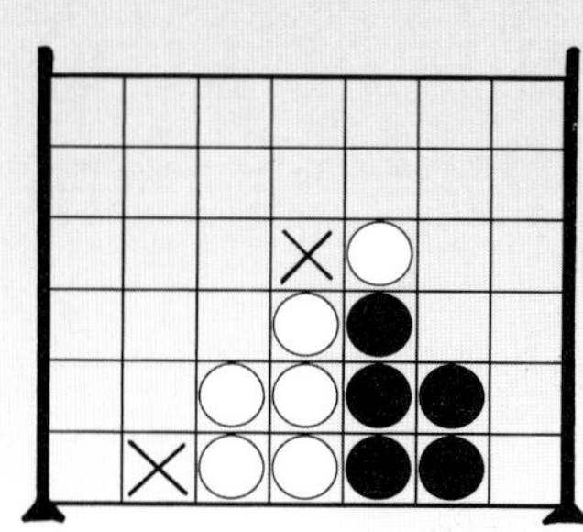

Shown at left is an example of clever strategy in the game "Four In a Row."

If you know the game, you can follow the skillful play of "White." "White" has placed his stones in such a way that he has two chances to get four in a row. (The squares are marked with an X.) Meanwhile, "Black" has only one chance to block the moves. "White" is sure to win.

Chess players are even more skilled in strategically clever play. They plan ahead for many moves, over several hours and even days, to set up a victory. They also use tactics; they distract their opponents, or make them uncertain, or send them on a false trail by well-thought-out sequences of moves.

Strategy and Tactics in Fencing

You have probably heard a coach say to one of his fencers after a bout, "You used great tactics!" Or he might say, "I thought we worked out a strategy. Why didn't you stick with it?" Have you ever wondered what the coach might mean by "tactics" or "strategy"? Is this something you need to know too?

Watch a bout between two good fencers and try to figure out what they do to defeat their opponent and why they probably do what they do:

The fencers watch each other with full concentration. No detail escapes them. If one stops paying attention for an instant, the other seized the opportunity to attack. They advance and retreat at varying speeds and with steps of varying length.

They try to intimidate the opponent or startle him. Suddenly one holds his weapon aside as if to say, "Come on, attack me." Sometimes they question the referee about why she decided a point one way and not another. Or they face each other without doing anything. Neither fencer makes a move. Why are they doing that?

Watching the fencers, the coach calls out advice:

All of that is known as "strategy" and "tactics." It includes creating favorable situations for you to score a touch, trying to guess your opponent's intentions while hiding your own, and tricking or outwitting your opponent. With strategy and tactics, you learn to use your technique and your condition in ways that help you defeat your opponent.

Naturally, you must observe the rules of competition as closely as you watch the behavior of your opponent.

Strategic and tactical fencing brings together well planned, thoughtful, clever, calculating, and even cunning behavior that helps you score points against your opponent and win your bout.

Strategy and tactics provide the vehicle for a fencer's cleverness. That's why people sometimes say that fencing is like chess with weapons. Careful observation, clever thinking, and lightning-quick decisions are crucial skills for a fencer.

The Elements of Strategy and Tactics

Knowledge

Fencing as a competitive sport is governed by conventions. Every fencer who sets out to engage in fair and safe competition with his opponent must abide by these agreements.

To underpin your fencing strategy, you must be very familiar with these conventions. You must know everything about the types of weapons, the target areas, the right of way, and all the rules of competition and specifications for weapons. Also, you must execute all your own movements and behaviors according to the rules.

For example, even as a beginner you learned that you must demand priority by extending your arm and continuously threatening the other fencer's target.

What Karl is telling Julie on the previous page is nonsense, of course. You knew that. Obviously, a fencer could use such rough-and-tumble methods to score against an opponent. But these points would not be valid in fencing competitions, because the behavior is against the rules.

In training, you learn the technical skills and information about sequences that lead to success according to the rules.

Plan Your Sequences in Advance

To improve your skill at executing quick, sure reactions, you should practice planning your moves in advance. In training sessions, you learn ways you can react to actions taken by your opponent.

For example:

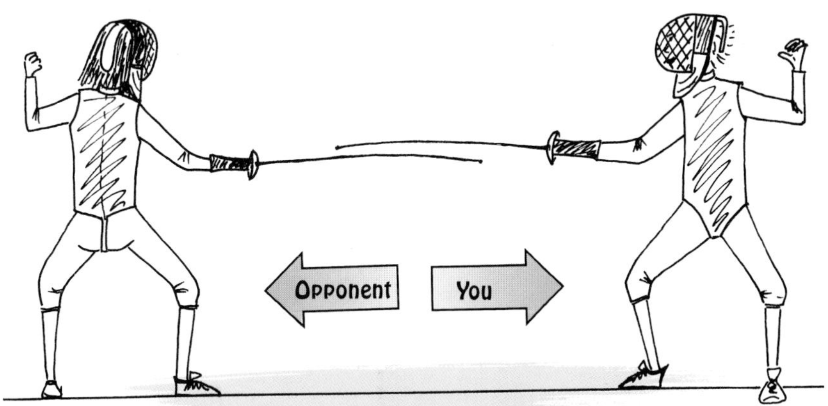

Opponent	You	
• advance	• retreat	______
• extended arm	• parry	______
• engaging your blade	• disengage	______
• invitation	• feint	______

Of course, there's more than one possible reaction to your opponent's actions.

Do you have other ideas? Write them on the lines above.

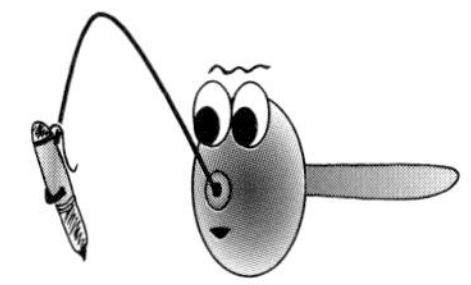

Now think through these sequences.

1. Fencing situation: Your opponent stands in invitation.

- *What attack could you make?* — *Direct attack*
- *How could your opponent respond?* — *Parry–riposte*
- *How could you plan your attack if you expect this response?* — *Feint*

2. Fencing situation: Your opponent touches or engages your blade.

- *What attack could you make?* — *Disengagement*
- *How could your opponent respond?* — *Parry–riposte or stop the attack*
- *How could you plan your attack if you expect this response?* — *Feint if parry–riposte; second intention if you stop the attack*

3. Fencing situation: Your opponent stands blade in line.

- *What attack could you make?* — *Sweep*
- *How could your opponent respond?* — *Parry–riposte or counter-riposte*
- *How could you plan your attack if you expect this response?* — *Attack if parry–riposte; second intention if counter-riposte*

You could expand on these sequences as much as you like. What's important is that in a bout, you are able to anticipate your opponent's responses. Then his actions won't come as a surprise, and you'll react much more quickly. You already knew what was coming.

Skills

When you sit comfortably on the couch and read the sequences on the previous page, it's easy to figure out the next action. But what about when you're actually fencing? Sweat is pouring down your face, you're all excited, and the actions are super-fast. Can you predict your opponent's action, your own reaction, and your opponent's response under those conditions? A good fencer must be able to do this!

A fencer must be able to think at lightning speed, recognize the situation, assess her opponent, and then make the right decisions in no time at all. It's true that a fencer must be as clever as a chess player, but she doesn't have the luxury of pondering for several minutes about her next move.

If someone were to attack you on the street, you would probably react spontaneously. You might push him away, grab his arm, leap to the side, or simply take to your feet and run away. These are possible ways to defend yourself, but in a fair fencing competition they are against the rules. For a fencing bout, you must develop other skills for defense and of course also for the attack.

As a fencer, you need to think on your feet. You must be able to take in a fencing situation immediately and decide on the right course of action. For this to happen, the sequences we described on the previous pages must run through your mind at lightning speed. Even as you are fencing, you must see that your actions are effective and you can continue, or recognize the need to change your approach because your actions are not working out as you planned.

Fairness

Look, your shoelace is untied.
Oh, thanks. Which one?
Gotcha! Ha, ha!

Tactical tricks are at the heart of fencing, but all tactics should be fair and follow the rules. Behavior like that shown at right is unsportsmanlike.

A good fencer must be able to think quickly and master technique, but above all he must know the rules of fencing, observe safety guidelines, and fight fair. This includes showing up with his equipment in perfect condition, accepting the decisions of the referee, and respecting his opponent.

Deceit, manipulation of technique, bribery, and doping have no place in the sport of fencing.

Wanted: Good Decisions

In fencing, victory goes to the fencer who makes the right decisions during a bout and can carry them out successfully. To make the right decision about the next actions, you must be aware of many things at once, taking them all in at the same time.

Chief among these are
- the distance
- the position of your opponent's weapon
- your opponent's movements.

You compare all of these against your experiences in many bouts.

Sometimes you can sense that your opponent is about to attack even before you see it. In the course of many bouts with different fencers, a good fencer stores up experiences that let her identify a fencing situation quickly and recognize what the opponent has in mind.

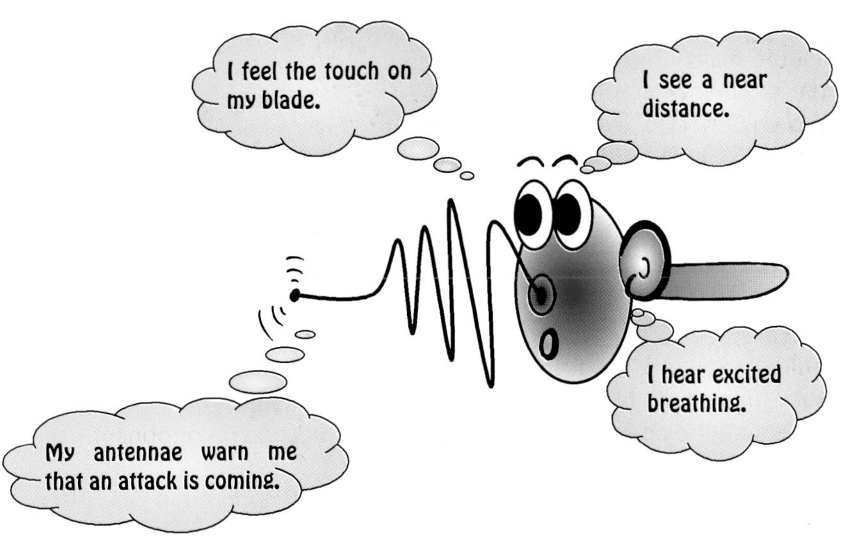

What can you do about this in training?

When you practice, fence seriously and with concentration. Learn to recognize a fencing situation and respond with the right action. Think about how your training partner could trick you by feinting or deception, and try not to fall into the trap.

But how does a fencer take in the entire fencing situation? Does he do this with his eyes, with his ears, or even with his muscle sense? Even the experts aren't sure, and certainly it varies from one athlete to another.

But one thing is certain: You can improve your perceptivity and decision-making ability by serious training. Seek out training partners who, like you, want to learn properly and improve their skills. Then training will be fun, and perhaps you will see results in your next competition. If not, be patient – keep working, and eventually you will be rewarded.

Even though you are no longer a novice, you are still learning. Perception, decision-making, reactions, and managing a fencing bout are complicated skills.

We will try to explain how they fit together by comparing them with riding a bicycle, which you probably learned a long time ago.

Riding a Bicycle	Fencing
To ride a bicycle, you need to keep your balance, pedal, and steer.	To fence, you need to learn the fencing stance, the advance and retreat, the lunge, the positions, and other techniques.
In addition, you need to know about traffic regulations, traffic signals, and how to ride in traffic.	A fencer must understand the conventions of the sport. These include safe equipment, the valid target area, the meaning of the lines on the strip, and what behavior is permitted or not permitted.
Then you must decide where you are going. At an intersection, you need to know whether you are turning left, turning right, or continuing straight ahead.	The "intersection" for a fencer is the fencing situation, such as distance, the opponent's behavior, and the position of weapons. You must know whether you want to (or should) attack, defend, or start a counterattack.
Finally, you have to pay attention to signs and signals. You need to know that a red light means stop, a green arrow means it's safe to turn, and a white arrow on the pavement tells which way traffic in that lane will flow.	The fencer must also understand the meaning of the distance, the blade position, the direction of movement, and the position, and recognize how these influence what he intends to do.

And now, you must practice, practice, practice...
A bicyclist must ride and ride.
A fencer must fence and fence!

The First Steps Are the Hardest

It's only logical that a novice fencer can't keep everything in view and also make all the right decisions. But with practice, you can learn. Soon you will recognize a situation and react almost automatically, without stopping to think.

Then you will simply have a sense of what is the right thing to do. Your coach no doubt talks about "distance sense," "blade sense," and "competition sense."

Strategy – The Right Plan Makes a Difference

Observing other fencers, you have surely noticed certain characteristics. One is very quick, another more hesitant. One doesn't think at all, but just pokes wildly around; another tries a prolonged distance game to bring his opponent within reach. There are tall fencers with long arms, right-handed and left-handed fencers, combative fencers and timid ones.

You'll hear young fencers ask their coach, "What should I do when I fight Tom? He's so much taller than I am!" Or, "Julia is so quick!" Or, "Why don't I ever beat Paul?" Of course, your coach will have ideas and suggestions for you. She has much more experience and knows more about fencing.

But for the sake of your own development as an athlete, it's important to begin thinking for yourself about how to win against a variety of opponents.

Think of an approach, and try it out. Of course, you will make some mistakes, but experience is the best teacher. Your coach will help you. Tell her what you plan to do, and listen to her advice.

What a Fencer Needs for Good Strategy and Tactics

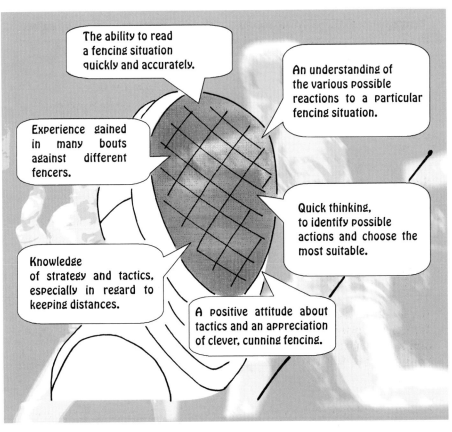

The ability to read a fencing situation quickly and accurately.

An understanding of the various possible reactions to a particular fencing situation.

Experience gained in many bouts against different fencers.

Quick thinking, to identify possible actions and choose the most suitable.

Knowledge of strategy and tactics, especially in regard to keeping distances.

A positive attitude about tactics and an appreciation of clever, cunning fencing.

Perceptivity and thinking are important for quick and correct decisions in a fencing bout. Take every practice bout seriously, to improve your perceptivity and thinking skills.

Be happy when your tactics work, and if they fail, just keep practicing!

Research – Maneuver – Conceal

Your goal is to score valid touches and to win your bout. Because you rarely reach this goal by direct action, you need strategy.

You must

- *Research*
  Get to know your opponent's strengths, weaknesses, and intentions.
- *Maneuver*
  Create favorable conditions and situations for your actions.
- *Conceal*
  Mislead your opponent. Don't let her know what you intend to do and what you can do.

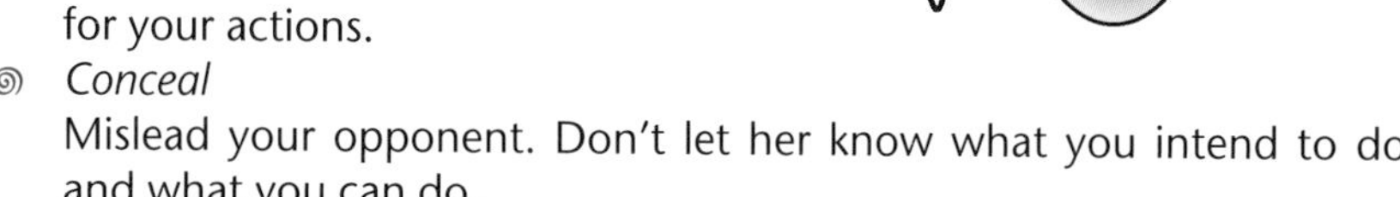

Examples of Strategic and Tactical Fencing

Example 1:

- You want to attack your opponent, but you don't know how she will respond. So you make a vigorous but brief attack. You don't really intend to attack; you just want to see how she reacts. You are only *researching* whether she gives way and how she parries. If she panics and goes right to a parry, a feint is possible.

- Now you initiate a distance game, in order to *maneuver* your opponent into a distance that is favorable for your feint.

- Of course, you can't let your opponent notice that you are preparing to attack and that this distance game is part of your plan. You act as if you don't want to attack; you *conceal* your true intentions.

When the right moment comes, you surprise your opponent from the same situation in which you used the feint in your research.

Example 2:
You notice that your opponent often extends his arm protectively and threatens you with his weapon. What is your strategic decision? That's right – sweep! You need an attack that pushes or strikes the opponent's weapon away before the thrust.

Now begins the *preparation*, getting ready for the attack.

You must research whether, when and how the opponent extends his arm and threatens you with his weapon.

Whether? It is important to see that the strategy is correct and that you have correctly observed your opponent's behavior.

When? It is important to find the right moment for the sweep. Let your opponent, not you, be taken by surprise.

How? It is important to decide what kind of sweep to use.

Now you take the initiative and determine the course of events. *Maneuver* your opponent into a distance that makes him vulnerable and determine the time at which he extends his arm.

But – so your opponent can't tell what you have in mind – you must *conceal* the timing and the nature of your attack (for example, quart–contact–thrust or sixte–beat–disengagement hit). To do this, you vary the distance game and blade game so that your opponent can't research your intent.

Be careful! Always keep the entire situation in view! Your opponent has also practiced strategy and tactics and most likely has read this book too!

So, now you can start! Try it in your next training bout or competition. Don't go to your coach to ask what you should do. Try it yourself, just the way you practiced in your training sessions.

Go for it! You can do it!

Exercise Your Thinking Skills!

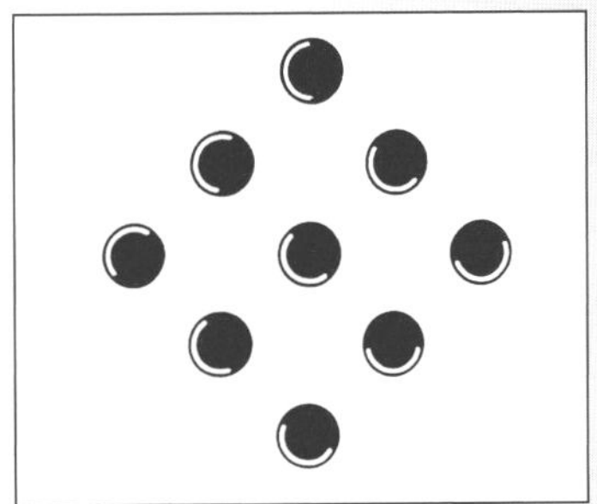

Connect these nine points with four straight lines in one continuous stroke.

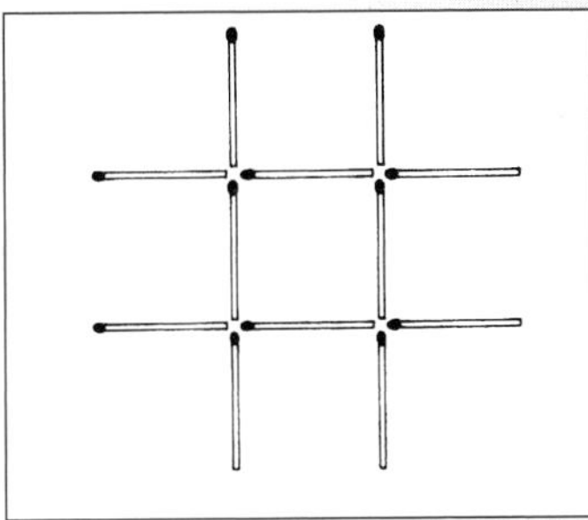

Move three matches to form just three squares of equal size.

A situation in a high mountain pass:

Goats cross the road.

But pictures A, B, C, and D at right are not in the proper order. In what order did the events shown in the pictures occur?

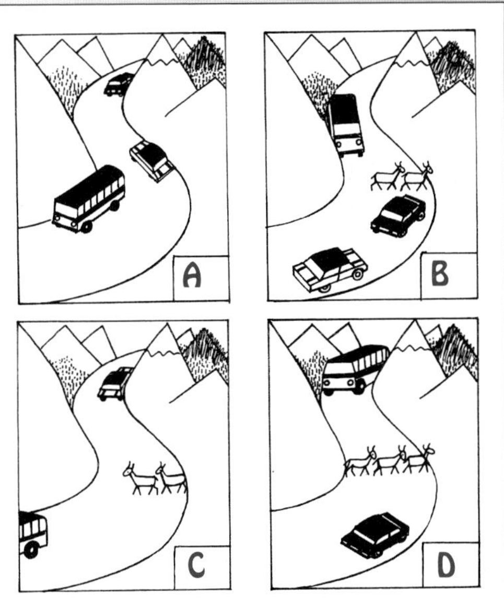

Test yourself!

For an evaluation of scores, see Chapter 13.

Situation: You don't feel like going to fencing practice today.

	Points
A. Of course, you stay at home, because you shouldn't have to practice if you don't feel like it.	1
B. You go to the fencing hall without enthusiasm, only because you don't want to disappoint your parents.	2
C. You go to practice as usual, because you fall behind if you miss a training session. Maybe it will be fun after all.	3

Situation: You need only one more touch to win this bout.

A. You concentrate and calmly plan your next action.	3
B. You think to yourself, "I've got him now," and you glance out of the corner of your eye to see whether your friends are watching.	2
C. You worry that you'll mess up somehow and lose after all.	1

Situation: For the team competition, you are named as a substitute.

A. You think to yourself, "Too bad. I probably wasn't good enough to make the team.	2

B. You're upset, because you are at least as good as the others. You hope the other team wins, so they'll realize they needed you. 1

C. You cheer for your team and set yourself a training goal: to be-selected for the team next time around. 3

Situation: In a bout, you notice that although your attack is good and your reactions are quick, you rarely score. Your thrusts are usually too short.

A. That makes sense; your opponent is taller and has longer arms. 1

B. You think about how you could use a distance game, faster steps and a longer lunge to get closer to your opponent. 3

C. You think, "Oh, well, maybe I'll be lucky and win anyway." 2

Situation: You notice that the judges awarded a touch to the wrong fencer. With this "assist," you could win faster.

A. You tell the referee that the score isn't right, because you want to earn your victory fairly. 3

B. You wait and see how the bout goes. You can always say something later. 2

C. You think, "Super! I hope nobody notices. Everybody deserves to get lucky now and then." 1

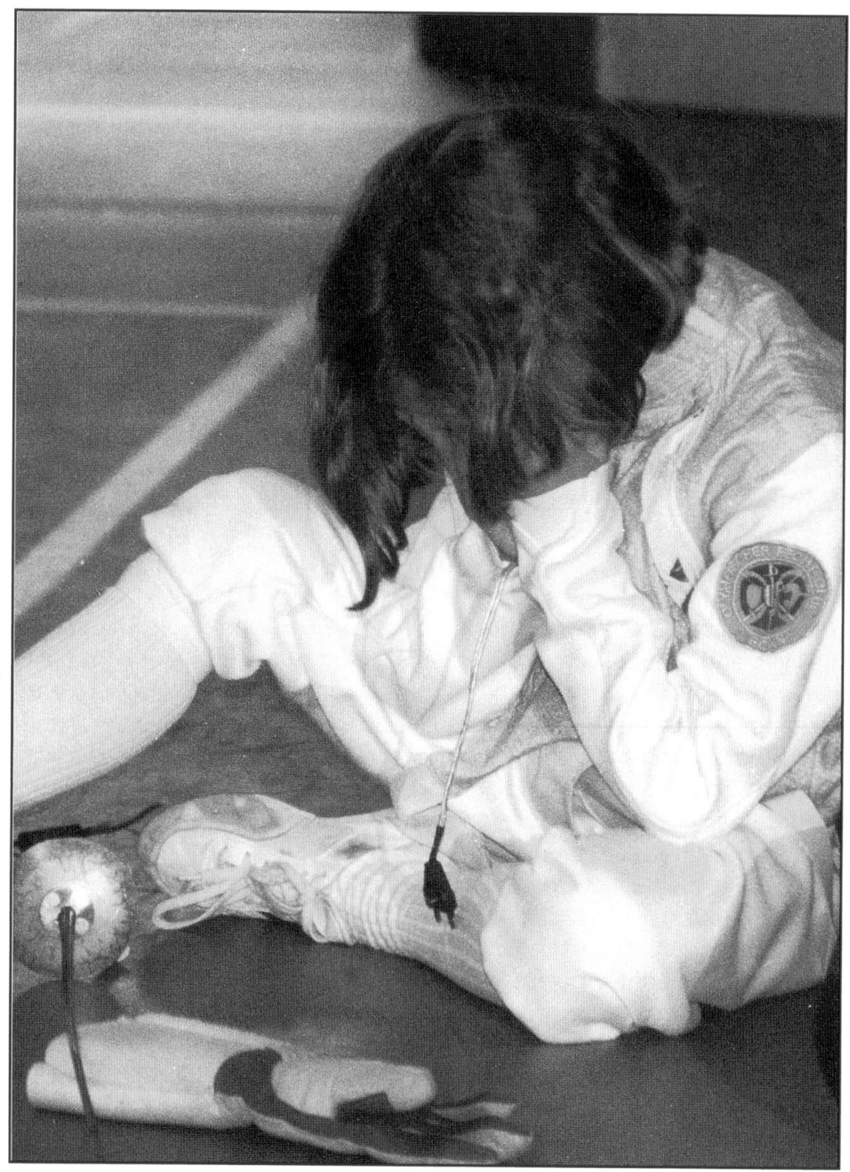

......................8 Psychological Skills

How does it happen that humans can feel joy and sorrow, that they fall in love or that they hate? How does it happen that humans can think, remember, and dream? We humans have always wondered what goes on inside our heads. When we couldn't explain it any other way, we simply called all of this the soul.

A prominent German physician, Rudolf Virchow (1821–1902), once challenged his students to find the soul in the human body. Yet when the students dissected cadavers, they found the brain, the heart, the lungs, the liver, and other organs – but no sign of the soul. They could not have found the soul by dissection. Perceiving and imagining, thinking and deciding, feeling and wanting are all activities carried out by the living brain. The branch of science that studies these activities is called *psychology*. Scientists today use the word *psyche* rather than soul to describe the mind as the center of thought, emotions, and behavior.

When we speak of psychological skills, therefore, we mean how the fencer can deal with pleasure, anger, frustration, desire, anxiety, and many other emotions, turning them to good use while fencing. Psychology also studies thought processes and how our muscles receive commands. We sometimes picture our brain as a computer that controls our entire body. When you are fencing, your "computer" is working at top speed, so it must be as well trained as your muscles.

What Does Our "Computer" Look Like Inside?

This is not a medical textbook. What's more, the human brain is much too complicated and broad a topic to cover in one chapter. But many people really think that sports are only about the muscles. They don't know that stimuli for the muscles come from the brain, or that every complicated athletic movement and behavior is controlled by nerve connections in the brain. We want you to understand how important your brain is in fencing, so we simply could not have left this chapter out of the book.

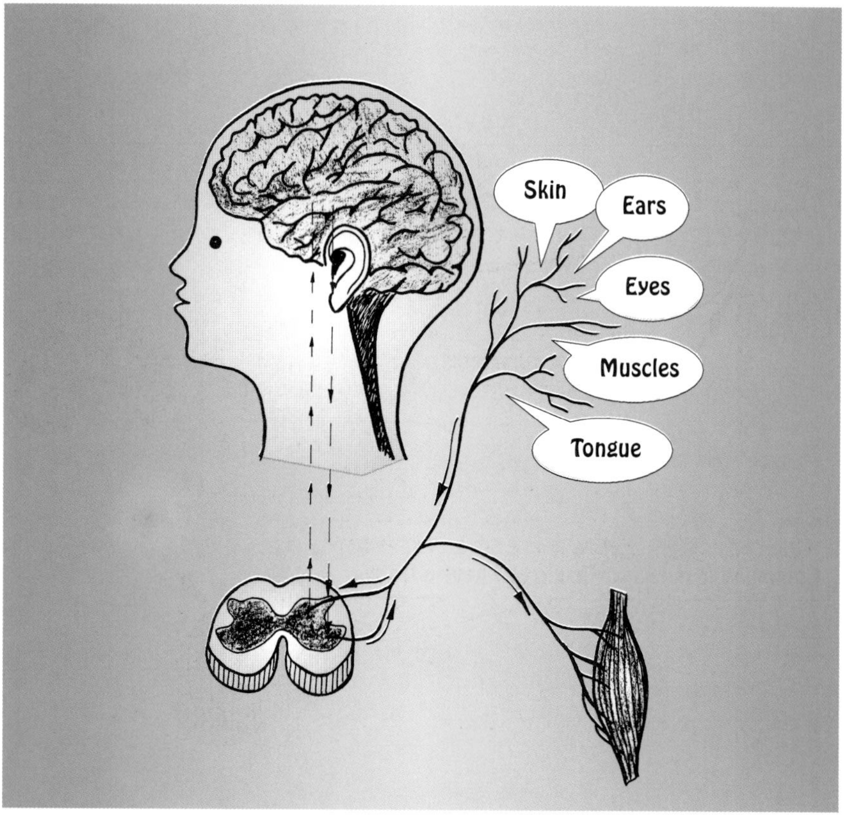

The Pathway of Perception – Relay – Brain – Muscle

In the drawing, you see a greatly simplified view of how this process works. Receptors in your sensory organs take in a great deal of information. You see, hear, taste, or feel. This information travels over nerve pathways to your brain. On the way, it passes through a "switchboard" of neurons in the spinal cord. (Our drawing depicts this as a cross section of the spinal cord.) The brain then announces to the particular muscles what action to take.

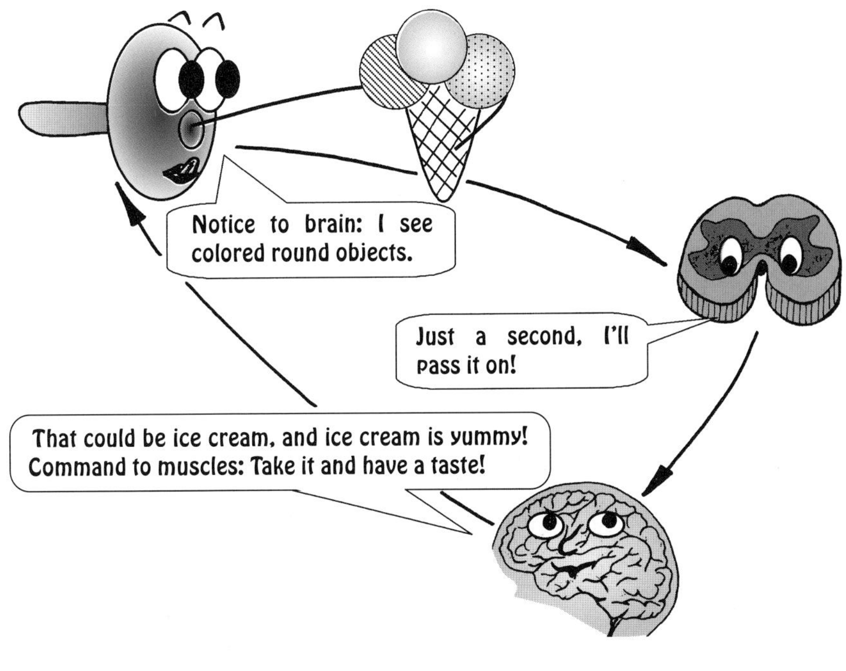

Reflexes

Do you recognize the following situations? Accidentally touching a hot burner on the stove, you instantly jerk your hand away. Blinded by a bright light, you close your eyes. Skidding on an icy sidewalk, you raise your arms to catch your balance.

In these situations, your muscles react on their own; you don't consciously think about what to do. These reactions are called reflexes. Because you don't have to think first, the information doesn't have to be transmitted to your brain. The stimulus goes directly from the central nervous system to the muscles.

Reflexes in Fencing

In fencing, for example, your reflexes are at work when you parry against a surprise attack. You must react quickly and don't have time to think. Reflexes enable a fencer to defend herself more quickly and reliably.

But you can also make use of an opponent's reflexes. With a beat or another sudden movement, the opponent defends himself reflexively. Because you have planned for this reaction, you can now touch him with a disengagement or second intention.

If you know that your fencing opponent executes such misleading movements, you must concentrate hard so you won't fall into his traps. But you could also pretend to fall into them, so that your opponent thinks you are easily misled. Meanwhile, you are actually prepared for his next actions.

A fencing example:
Your opponent makes a four beat against your en garde position. You go immediately as if by reflex to a four parry. By doing this, you tempt your opponent into a four beat disengagement, which of course you can parry, because you were ready for it.

Conscious Reactions

Most of the stimuli and information we take in through our senses are transmitted by the association neurons to the relevant part of the brain. After receiving the message, the brain compares them with past experiences and processes them. The commands for conscious action are sent by the cerebral cortex through the spinal cord to the muscles.

Another fencing example:

Incoming stimulus:
The opponent attacks in earnest.

- *Comparison with experience:*
  He has done this many times before, and each time was a feint.

- *Conscious planning:*
  React as if to parry, but be ready to parry the disengagement right away.

Not easy! Don't worry; most of this will come if you train correctly. But these examples do illustrate the complicated workings of our on-board computer.

Plenty of partner exercises during practice and many bouts against different opponents train you to react quickly. As you accumulate experiences, you develop your reflexes.

These examples also give you an idea of how important it is to learn as much as you can about the sport of fencing. A fencer can decide much more quickly what a particular stimulus means and what is the best reaction to it if he is prepared and doesn't need to take time for conscious thought.

Psychological Strengths

Some folks say, "Confidence is half the battle." Of course, it's not that simple, but there is some truth to this. The person who approaches a task in a spirit of cheerful poise naturally has a better chance of success than a person burdened by worry and doubts.

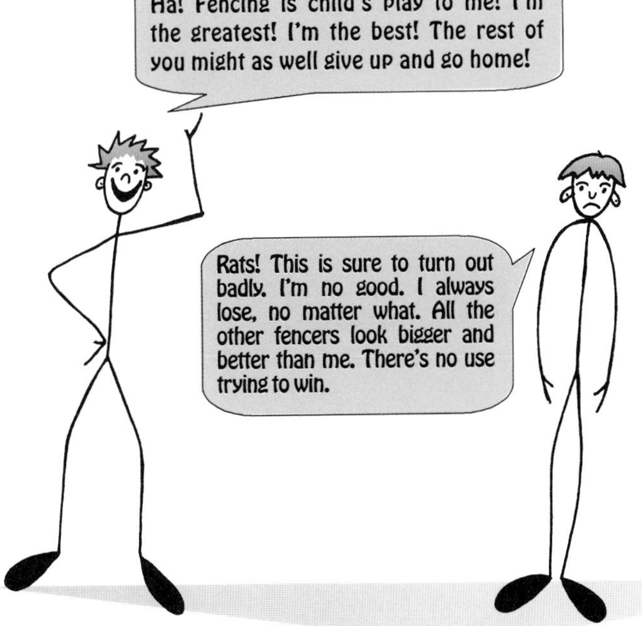

Ha! Fencing is child's play to me! I'm the greatest! I'm the best! The rest of you might as well give up and go home!
Rats! This is sure to turn out badly. I'm no good. I always lose, no matter what. All the other fencers look bigger and better than me. There's no use trying to win.

Of course, you shouldn't get arrogant and make mistakes because you were too self-confident.

Which of the following qualities are useful to a fencer, and which are a disadvantage? Cross out the qualities you don't want to have.

Self-confidence, enjoyment of fencing, self-doubt, blind rage, willingness to take risks, worry about losing, ambition, the will to win, trust in your own abilities, pessimism, moodiness, ability to concentrate.

Requirements for Successful Competition

Physical Fitness

You have trained well; you feel strong and limber, relaxed and full of energy. You have a good feeling about competing; you're a little excited, but not worried or nervous.

Mental Fitness

You're looking forward to your bouts and you want to win. You are sure that you will achieve your goal, but you're not anxious about losing.

A Winner's Attitude

You think positively and are optimistic. If you make a mistake, you don't give up; instead, you focus on winning.

A Winner's Posture

Look at these two fellows. Which one looks more likely to come out the winner? You're right – the one standing tall and confident. Show your opponent that you have confidence in yourself, even if something doesn't go your way.

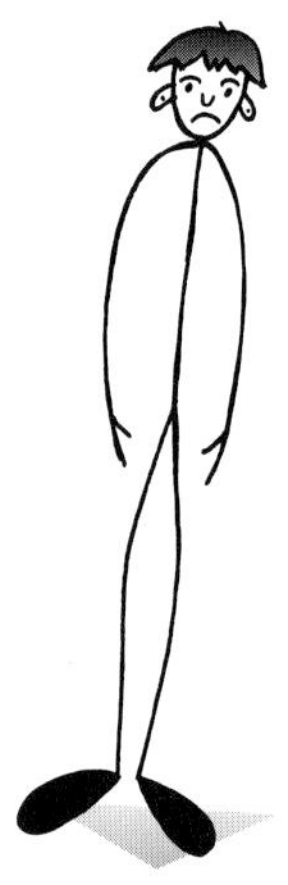

Tips for Competition

Reaction after you score a touch

- Pump your fist: "Yeah!"
- Allow yourself a quick celebration and praise yourself: "All right!" "Keep it up!"

Reaction after your opponent scores a touch

- Try to forget your error as quickly as you can and concentrate on the next action.
- Don't let your irritation show. Step away and take a deep breath.
- Turn around; jog two or three steps in place.
- Tell yourself "That's okay!" "Let it go!"

Relaxation when the bout is interrupted

- Go calmly to the start position. Tell yourself, "Stay calm." "Relax."
- Ways to relax: Inspect your plug or weapon; adjust your mask; pull up your socks.
- Take your time, but don't annoy the referee by deliberately delaying the bout.

Preparation after the bout is interrupted

- Visualize the next action or the next tactical move.
- Show in your posture and gestures that you are confident and ready to fence.
- Use small rituals, like flexing your blade once or twice, shaking out your arms, bouncing in place, and observing your opponent closely.

Watch the way strong and successful fencers relax and concentrate between touches and during pauses. Try to imitate them and figure out which methods feel comfortable to you. Practice these rituals and try to make a habit of using them.

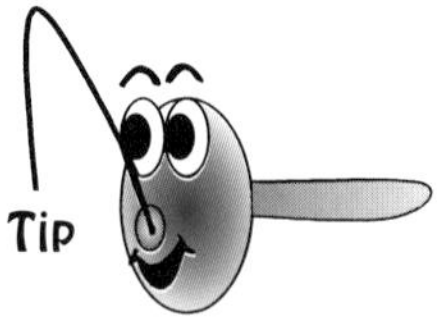

It often helps to make little speeches to yourself.

Tip

I'm going to win today!
Concentrate!

Stay calm –
you can do it.

Look at the way he's standing. I can tell he's afraid of me.

My parents are watching.
I'll show them what I can do!

Okay,
here we go!

Even the Best Fencers Lose Sometimes

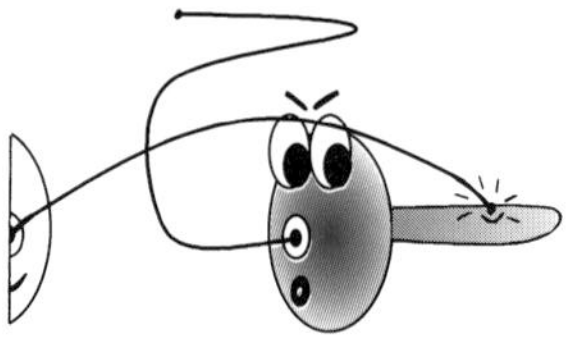

If you lose, you must ask yourself whether your expectations of winning were justified. Were you fencing against a much older and more experienced athlete? Then don't let it bother you; just keep on training. If you're good, someday you'll catch up with her. Be happy every time you score a point, and set yourself realistic goals for such bouts.

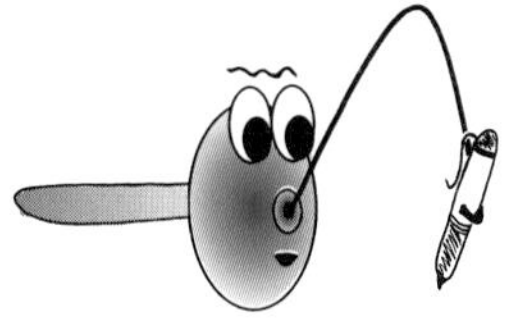

Think about why you lost. It helps to keep a record of your losses and the lessons you learned.

When did I lose? To whom?	Why I lost.	What will I do about it?
May 2 – Lucas	I missed on all my thrusts.	Practice thrusts.
June 10 – Tina	I couldn't parry her direct attacks.	I must be too slow; I can't keep the right distance. I'll talk to the coach about it.

Attention Span

Your attention span is the length of time that you can concentrate fully on one activity. Experience shows that attention spans vary with age.
Keep in mind that each person is different, and a person's attention span can also vary from day to day. Furthermore, during a competition the level of concentration is much higher; as a result, the length of time you can concentrate is much shorter.

Age:		
	5–7 years	about 15 minutes
	7–10 years	about 20 minutes
	10–12 years	about 25 minutes
	12–15 years	about 30 minutes

Ability to Concentrate

Learn to concentrate and stay alert!

Outside the window, the first snowflakes of winter drift down. Tom and Tina are arguing again. Across the fencing hall, a weapon clatters to the floor. Don't let yourself be distracted! During a training session or a competition, set aside all thoughts about problems at school or plans for next Saturday night. The more difficult the task, the harder you must concentrate. In fencing, everything happens at lightning speed. One lapse in concentration, no matter how brief, can allow your opponent to score.

Tips for improving your ability to concentrate

You have to want to pay attention!

If you're not really interested in that homework assignment, any little thing can distract you. You wonder what your friends are doing, watch a bird flitting past your window, listen to every noise in the house. That's no way to get your homework done! Before you concentrate, tell yourself why the task is important and what good it will do you.

Don't let anyone or anything distract you!

Think of your mind as a spotlight focused on a single point. Only that point is illuminated; everything else is dark. Concentrate on your fencing partner or your opponent. The minute you glance aside to see what's going on in the bout next to you, you have lost your focus. Even thinking about what would happen if you won the next point is a distraction. You aren't concentrating on your fencing.

Take a break now and then!

Your ability to concentrate is not infinite. Everybody needs opportunities to rest and recover from time to time.

Test Your Concentration

The beetle on the left is in love with the beetle on the right. He must crawl along the ribbon to reach his sweetheart. Will he actually reach her, or will he end up on the other side of the ribbon?

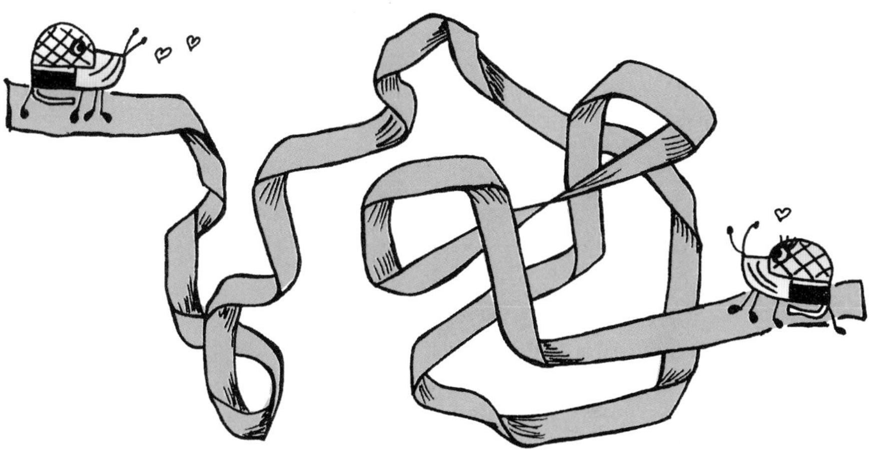

Relaxation

Concentration and relaxation are closely related. Only the person who truly relaxes before concentrating on a task and during any pauses can fully concentrate. To avoid making mistakes in a training session or a competition, a fencer must know how to relax.

Every fencer should learn a few different ways to relax. It's a good idea to try them out and practice them not only in sports, but in everyday situations as well.

Each fencer finds ways to relax that work for him. Try this method:

- *Sit or lie down.*
- *Close your eyes and take deep slow breaths.*
- *Inhale through your nose. Breathe deeply. Feel your abdomen rise.*
- *Exhale slowly through your mouth.*
- *Concentrate on your breathing and on your body.*

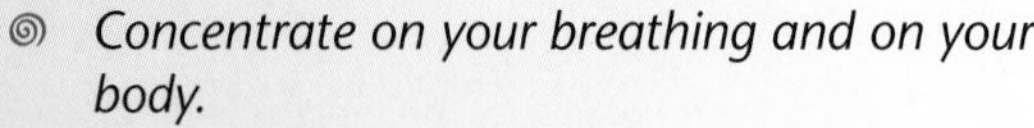

- *Let any other thoughts float away.*
- *Continue until you feel completely relaxed.*
- *Open your eyes and gently shake your arms and legs.*

Pressure That You Choose Builds Psychological Strength

What do you think about the following story?
Does it sound familiar to you?

> Max has been looking forward to the tournament. He told his family and friends how well his training sessions were going and that the competition was coming up. The night before the big day, Max packs his duffel bag and checks each item off his list. Now he just needs to go to bed early and get a good night's sleep.
>
> On the morning of the competition, everything still looks good. But when his first bout starts, suddenly nothing goes right. Movements he can do in his sleep go awry. His legs quiver. Every time his opponent feints, he falls for it. He is beside himself.
>
> All the spectators look at each other with the same question. What's up with Max?

What has happened to Max happens even to topnotch fencers in big, important tournaments. The pressure is just too much; he can't perform at his true level of ability.

It's not so bad, but annoying. You have to know why this situation can arise and what you can do against it.

Pressure Arises Out of Expectations.

Some expectations are external. They come from your parents, your coach, the members of your fencing club, and your friends. All these people expect you to perform well.

Bravo!
You're the best!
We're proud of you.
You're sure to win today.
Show them all what you can do!
I'm counting on you!

I really want to win today. I'll show everyone! I've been training hard – it's bound to pay off. Everyone will be proud of me.

And then there are the expectations you place on yourself. You have set certain goals, and you want to achieve them.

Sometimes, the pressure of these expectations gets to be too much. You start to worry that you won't be able to meet the high expectations that you or others have set. That causes stress!

Some Tips for Dealing with Pressure

- In your training sessions, prepare thoroughly for competition. Make a list of what you'll bring to the competition site. Get a good idea of the challenges you will face. That way, you won't be taken by surprise. Think of it as like getting ready for a test in school.

- You can choose your own level of pressure. Set your own goals and decide for yourself what you want to achieve. Of course, you could set goals that are easy to reach. You could sidestep the pressure by fencing only against weaker opponents, or not entering any tournaments at all. But would that benefit you? Set goals that are high, but realistic. A certain amount of pressure is good for you. It motivates you, keeps you working, and actually adds to the fun.

- Set aside any problems that have nothing to do with fencing. When you don your mask, tell yourself that no outside problems can get to you. From that point on, you will concentrate only on yourself and your opponent.

- Pressure builds character!
  Just as nature forms precious stones through heat and pressure, so your psychological abilities develop to competitive mettle only when you meet and master situations that involve pressure. With each effort, you become stronger. The athlete who makes a habit of avoiding pressure will become a weakling and will always fall short of his true abilities. The athlete who masters himself under pressure strengthens his character.

The qualities of character that you develop in training bouts and fencing competitions will also serve you well in other areas of life!

Test of Perception

Look at the picture below for ten seconds (count to ten). Cover the picture with your hand. Try to answer the questions on page 117 only from memory. Write the answers on the lines provided.

You can play this game of perception with your friends or family members. Use another picture, or the view out a window, or an entire room. After a short period of observation, blindfold one player while the other asks questions.

Which fencer is lunging, the one on the right or the one on the left?

Where does the touch land?

Who is wearing the armband?

How many replacement weapons are lying on the strip?

Does the replacement weapon have a French grip or an orthopedic grip?

What time is it?

Is the clock square or round?

Does the fencer on the left have a ponytail or braids?

Which fencer is wearing dark shoes?

Are the fencing gloves dark or light?

How many cables are visible on the scoring device?

Which lamp on the scoring device is lit?

Describe the man at the scoring device!

Now uncover the picture and check your answers. This was not an easy exercise! How much were you able to observe in just ten seconds?

..............9 Movements and Positions

During your first years as a fencer, you learned the basic techniques of fencing. By now, you know the basic position, the salute, the proper fencing position, and the advance and retreat, as well as the lunge and the recovery from the lunge. In addition, you have already learned three positions for the foil, the epee, and the saber. With this knowledge, you can already engage in real fencing bouts.

Like every novice fencer, you have surely had some difficulty with performing the movements well, and you have practiced them again and again. You have probably found this boring at times; you may have thought to yourself, "What's the big deal about perfect technique? What really matters is scoring!" In a way, that's true. But as you know, the special techniques of fencing have been developed over many years of fencing as a sport, and they have proven to be the most effective.

These include the deep fencing position, from which the fencer can move nimbly and easily; the special way to hold the grip, which allows you to handle the weapon skillfully and safely; and the quick lunge, which permits a lightning-fast attack.

At this point in your fencing career, however, you should no longer have to think about the best grip or the proper position of your weapon; instead, you must concentrate on your opponent, on attacks and parries. You must know the techniques as if in your sleep.

Of course, your training sessions will still include practicing movements, and your coach will continue to give you advice on how to improve them. That's right and proper.

Even if you're no longer a novice fencer, you will still be learning new techniques. On the next several pages, we describe additional leg movements and positions of the weapon.

Take a look at the drawing. Do the coach's comments and suggestions sound familiar to you? In the blank bubbles, write in the comments you hear most often as your coach corrects your technique.

The Jump

Like the step and the lunge, the jump is a leg movement to alter the distance between the fencers. Advanced fencers should practice it repeatedly in their training sessions. This promotes speed and the coordination of the arm and leg movements.

The special feature of the forward jump is that, as in the advance, the foot of the lunge leg begins the movement, but at the end of the jump both feet return to the floor at the same time.

Rear leg pushes off. Forward leg advances quickly. Jump low across the floor. Land in the fencing position.

Executing the forward jump:

- The bent forward leg advances powerfully; immediately, the rear leg pushes off vigorously.
- The fencer leaps forward, staying low to the floor.
- During the jump, the legs resume the fencing position.
- The fencer lands in the proper fencing position, with both feet touching down at the same time. The feet land flat on the floor.

When is the jump used?

- In combination with the lunge in a rapid attack from a wide distance.
- To startle the opponent with a swift movement, leading him into a careless reaction.

Typical errors to avoid:

The jump is too high. This makes the blade movement too unsteady. This isn't a high-jump contest – the goal is to advance at top speed.

Here, the fencer lands first on his forward leg. He will need far too much time for the next movement, such as a lunge.

Balestra – Forward Jump and Lunge

The international term for the combination of forward jump and lunge is *balestra.*

These two leg movements are executed without a pause. Only the fencer who lands in the correct fencing position with the right distribution of weight will be able to go immediately into a lunge. This very difficult combination takes a good deal of practice.

The goal of the balestra is to surprise the opponent with the speed of the attack.

Fleche – the Running Attack

The fleche is a sudden forward movement, like a sprinter taking off. The fencer pushes off vigorously with her legs and is momentarily off balance.

The initial movement can occur in different ways. After the takeoff, the lunging leg moves in front of the rear leg. The fencer regains her balance as she comes to a stop.

Positions of the Weapon

On the next few pages, we will review the positions you already know and describe two additional positions for the foil and epee and two for the saber.

Positions with foil and epee

Beginning fencers usually start by learning these three positions for the foil and epee:

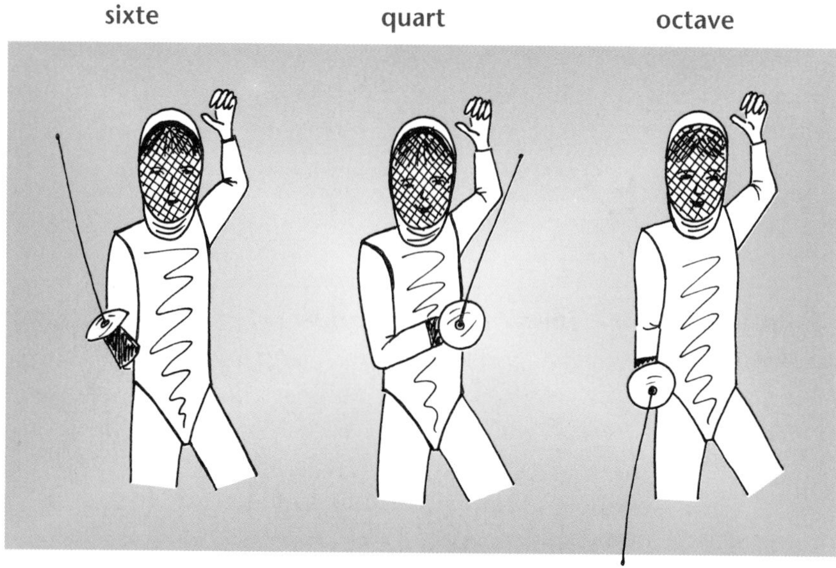

- Sixte is the position that covers the outside high line.
- Quart is the position that covers the inside high line.
- Octave is the position that covers the outside low line.

Prime

This position is on the left if you are right-handed, on the right if you are left-handed. The arm is somewhat bent and is held horizontally in front of the body.

The hand is pronated (held as if you were slicing bread) and about level with the rear shoulder. The tip of the blade is forward and down, level with the knee.

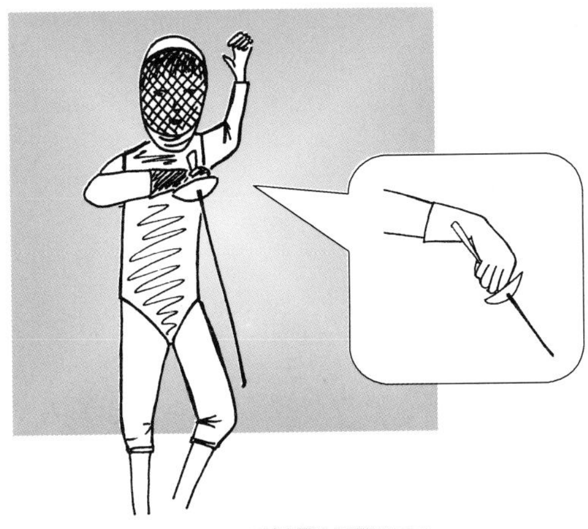

Avoid these errors when taking the prime position:

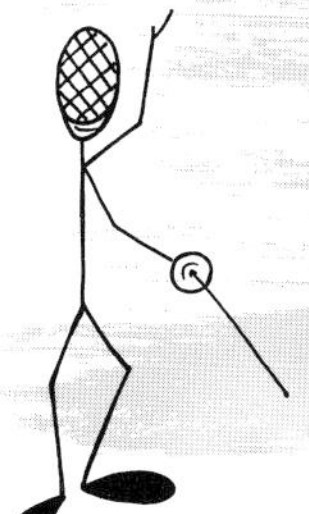

The hand is too low and the weapon is held much too far to the outside.

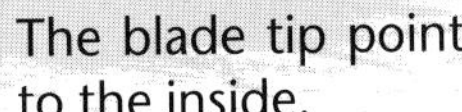

The blade tip points to the inside.

Septime

This position is like prime, but on the left. The arm is somewhat bent and the hand at chest level. The fist is turned slightly, supinated (as if you were holding a soupspoon). The blade tip is at thigh level, forward and down to the inside.

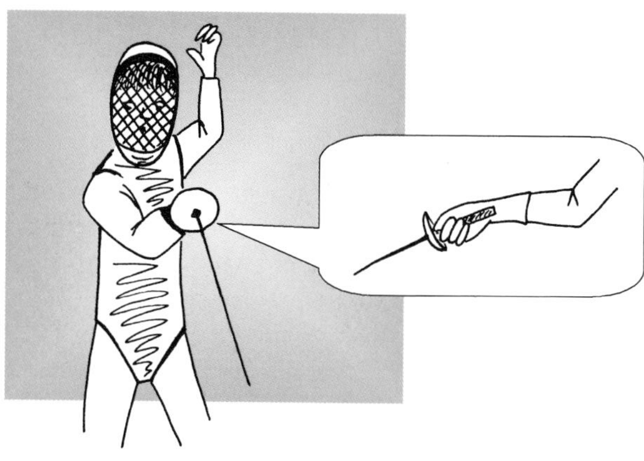

Avoid these errors when taking the septime position:

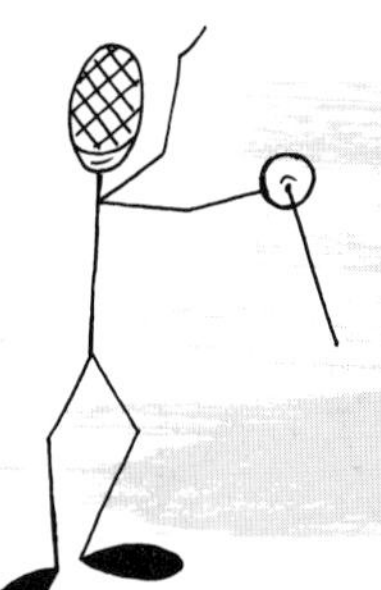

The position is extended far too much over the threatened target area.

The blade tip points down and to the outside, so that a complete defense is impossible.

Changes of Position

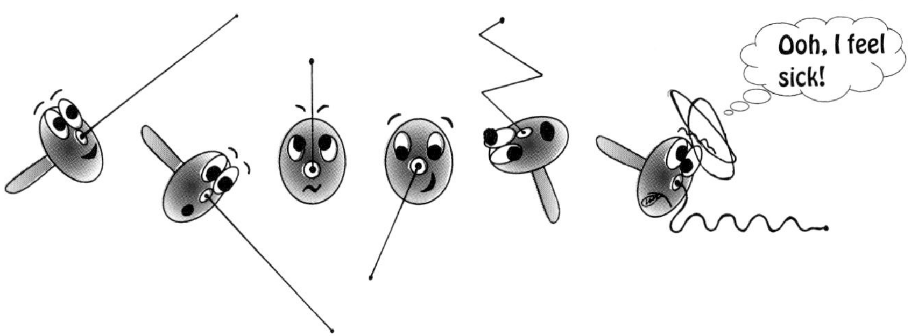

To change the position of your weapon, you use your arm, hand, and fingers. Depending on the starting and ending positions, the movement is direct, semicircular, or circular. With each change of position, the corresponding parts of the target area are opened or closed.

The direct change of position

The weapon and the arm are moved vertically or horizontally. Examples are the transition from

septime to quart

or

quart to septime

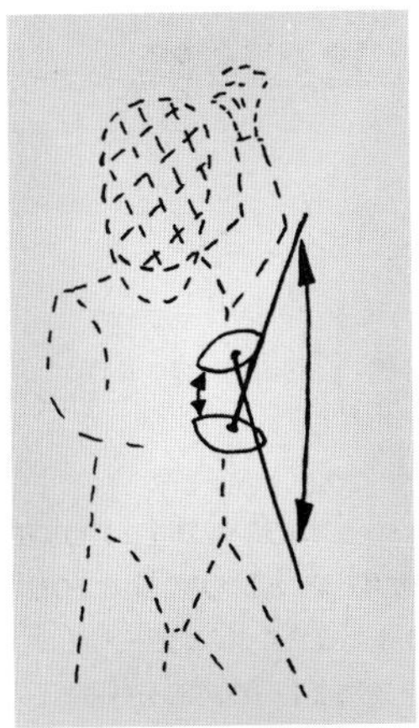

septime to octave

or

octave to septime

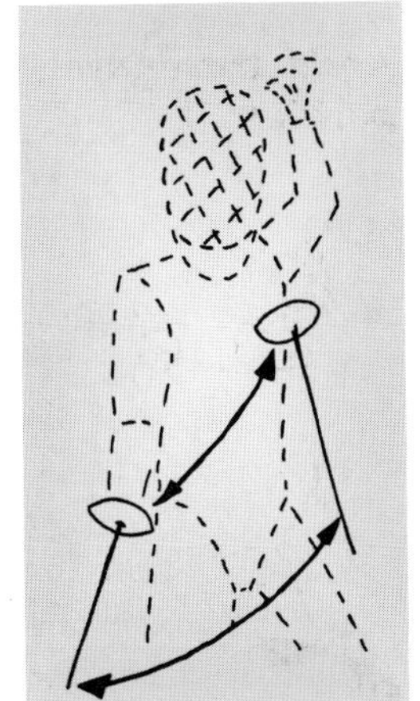

The semicircular change of position

Here, the change of position is diagonal. Examples include the transition from septime to sixte or from sixte to septime.

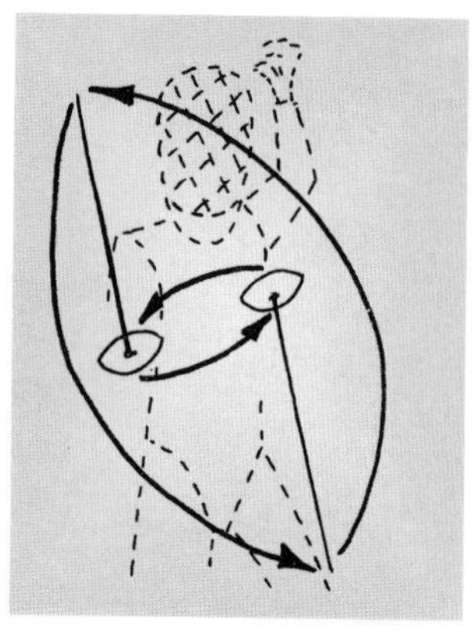

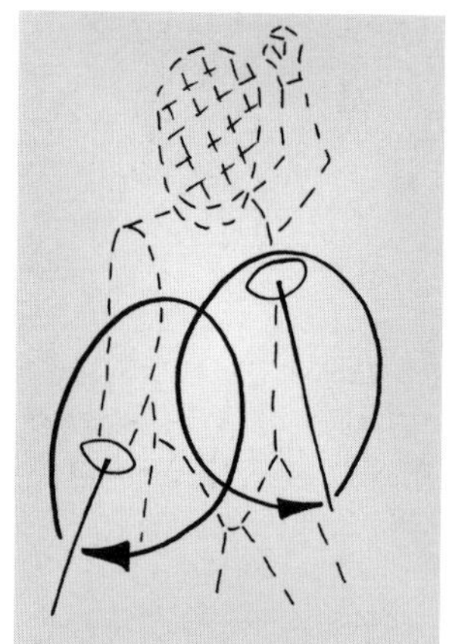

The circular change of position

The transition is made by turning the arm, the hand and the weapon in a circular movement. The drawing shows the transition from octave to octave and from septime to septime.

When changing position, think of the "muscle sense" we described in Chapter 6. Feel whether you have assumed the position correctly, so that the blade of your opponent is firmly engaged or the relevant target area is well protected.

With your weapon (or a pole), practice the individual positions at home. Your goal should be to assume each position quickly and precisely, as well as to move securely from one position to another.

- *Practice changes of position in front of a mirror.*
- *Close your eyes, assume a position, open your eyes, and check your stance in the mirror.*

For secure movement of the weapon, you can repeat the following exercises again and again:

- *With the tip of your blade, draw large and small figure eights in the air.*

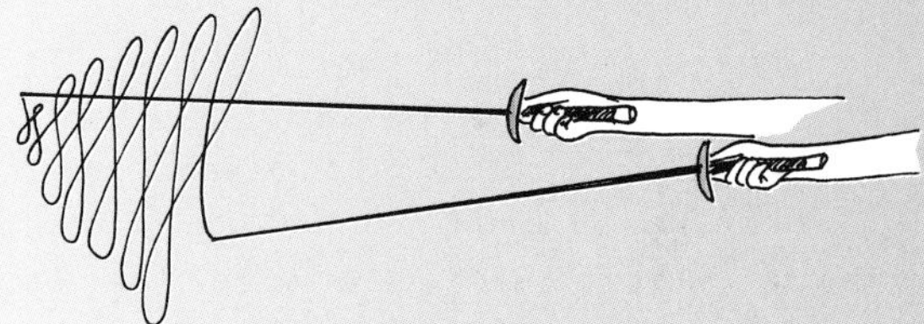

- *Draw spirals with the tip of the blade.*
- *Write your name in the air.*
- *Write words and have your partner guess what you wrote.*

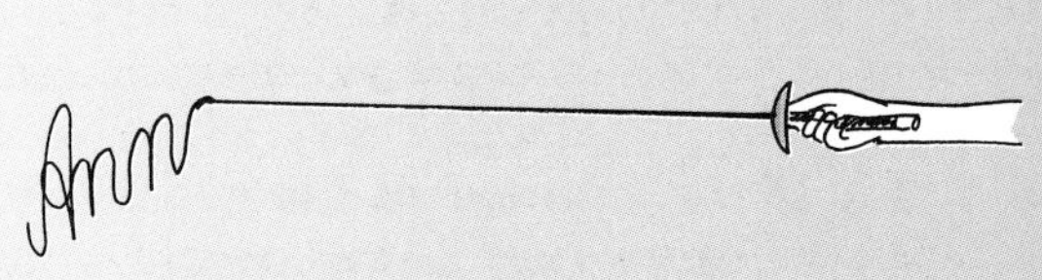

Positions with the Saber

For fencing with the saber, you probably started by learning the following positions:

third quint quart

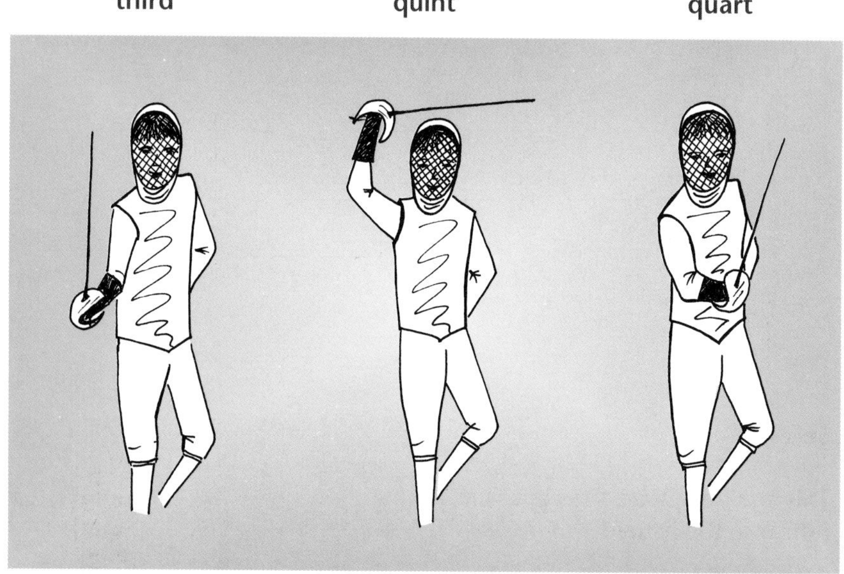

- Third is the position that protects against an outside cut to the flank.
- Quint is the position that protects against a cut to the head.
- Quart is the position that protects against a cut to the chest.

In these positions as well, take care to move your weapon only as far as necessary to protect the threatened target area.
Your hand is turned properly if the edge lies toward the expected cut.

Prime

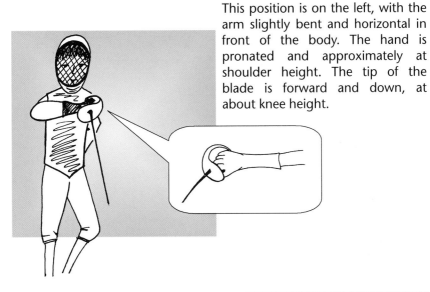

This position is on the left, with the arm slightly bent and horizontal in front of the body. The hand is pronated and approximately at shoulder height. The tip of the blade is forward and down, at about knee height.

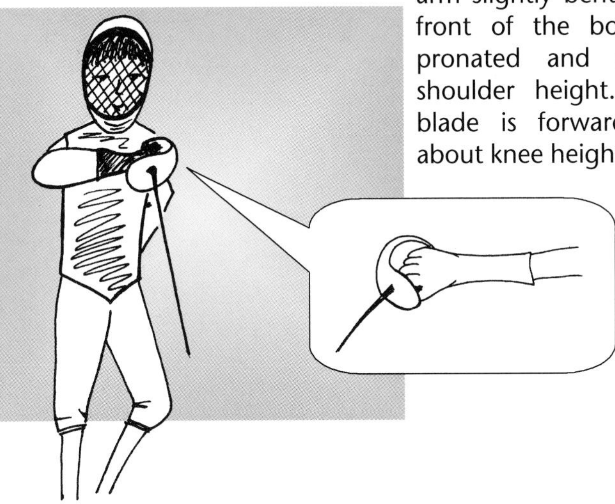

Second

This position is on the right and is similar to the octave.

The arm is very slightly bent, the hand pronated and about even with the pelvis.

The tip of the blade is forward and down, about thigh-high.

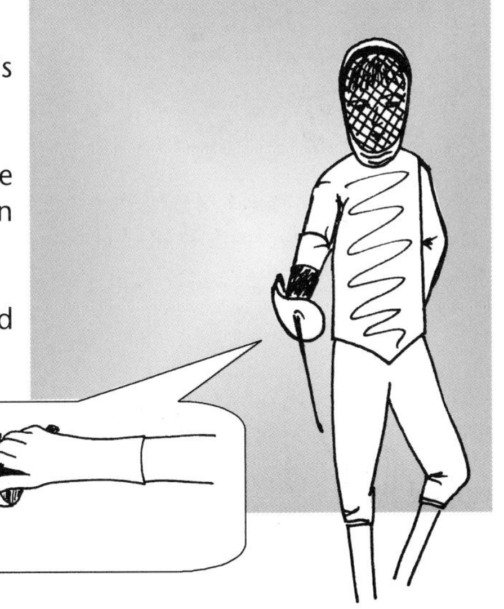

Changes of Position with the Saber

Here we show some changes of position with the saber. As with the foil and epee, you change the position of the weapon for an invitation, contact, or parry. In the drawings, you can see that there are often different ways to move from one position to another. Your choice depends on your intention and the position of your opponent's blade.

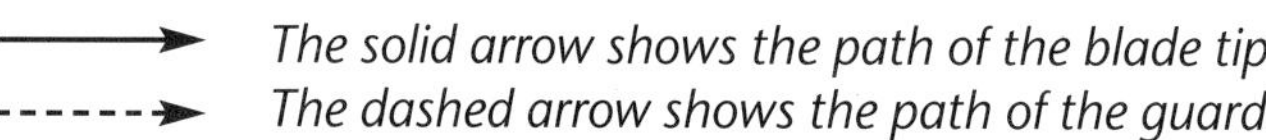

The solid arrow shows the path of the blade tip.
The dashed arrow shows the path of the guard.

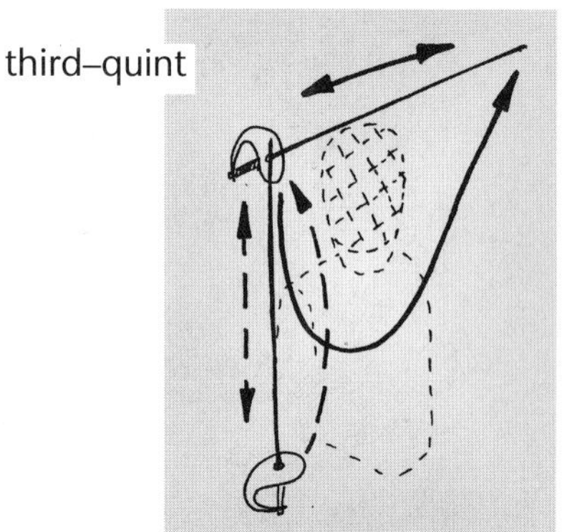

quint–quart

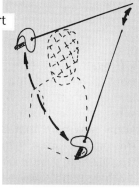

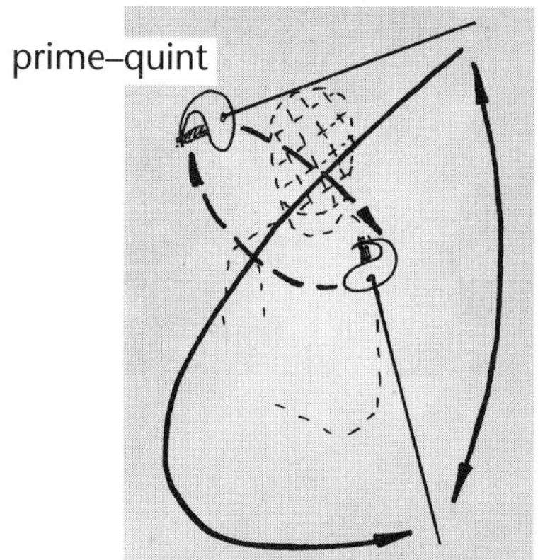

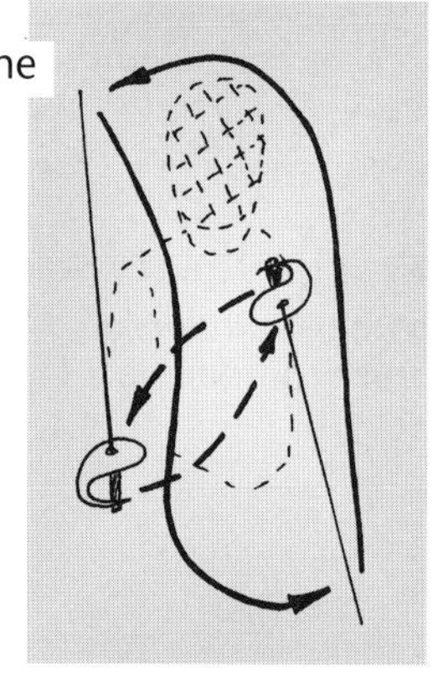

10 The Electronic Scoring Device

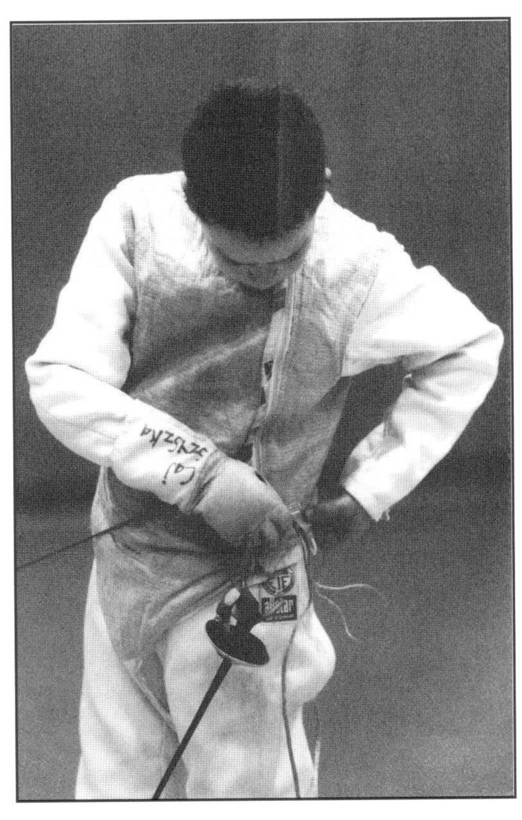

I can still remember my own days as a fencer. In the beginning, we didn't have an electronic scoring device for training bouts and smaller tournaments. Two line judges stood on each side of the strip. Their job was to observe the bout closely and tell the referee when and where they saw a touch. You know how hard that is to do, and you can imagine how often there were disagreements about their decisions.

Trickery was not unknown in those days. After receiving a valid touch in a saber bout, a fencer might suddenly rub wildly at his thigh and grimace as if in pain.

The observer would assume that the touch struck the fencer's thigh and therefore was invalid. An electronic scoring device would not have been so easily fooled.

Fortunately, almost all fencing bouts today are electronic. But the electronic systems have their own quirks, and beginners in particular may have a hard time understanding them. In this chapter, we want to help you learn more about the electronic scoring device and perhaps explain it to your friends, parents, or grandparents as well. The drawings in this book are greatly simplified. If you are interested in more details, consult other publications, or ask your coach or your club's technical advisor.

It is also important to know that the electronic scoring device is being developed further. For example, it will not be long before even cordless fencing is so highly developed that the cable spools are no longer needed.

Hurray, the light went on!

A fencing bout can be so swift and complex that many spectators don't know what has happened until the light goes on. But the electronic scoring device does more than help fans follow a bout; it also supports the work of the referee.

The white and colored lights show:

- Who has made a touch.
- Whether the valid target area was touched.
- Whether the touch was invalid.
- For the foil and epee, whether the thrust had the necessary force.
- In foil, whether an invalid touch was made before the valid touch.

The electronic scoring device can give us all this information. This makes fencing matches much more fair and makes the referee's task easier.

How an Electronic System Works

The **foil system** works on a closed circuit, like your doorbell at home. The tip of the foil is like the button outside the door. If the tip touches the woven metal vest with sufficient pressure, the colored light goes on; if the touch is outside the valid target area, the white light goes on. The metal strip and the guard are connected in such a way that a touch on them is not recorded.

The **saber system** also works on a closed circuit. Like the foil fencer, the saber fencer wears a special garment made of woven metal that covers the valid target area. For the saber fencer, this includes not only the torso, but also the arms and the mask.

The system must be connected in such a way that a stab or cut with the blade closes the contact with the metal vest, thus turning on the light.

The **epee system** works on an open circuit. The entire body is a valid target area, so no special metal clothing is required. Here too, the guard and the strip are connected in such a way that a touch on them does not show.

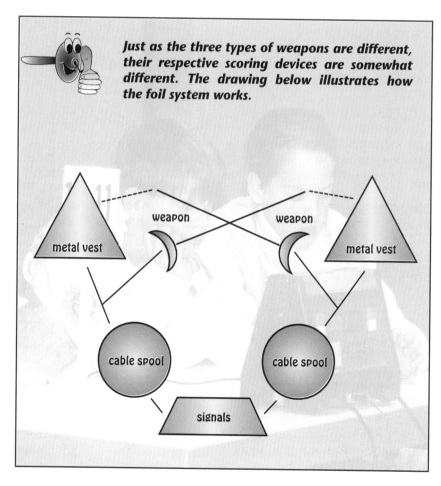

Just as the three types of weapons are different, their respective scoring devices are somewhat different. The drawing below illustrates how the foil system works.

weapon
weapon
metal vest
metal vest
cable spool
cable spool
signals

What Matters Is the Tip

Remember, today's sport of fencing had its origins in serious life-or-death battles. In the olden days, the fencer had to strike with force to have any effect. A light touch would mean nothing.

The rules of today follow the same principle. Only a touch executed with a minimum force is valid.

The tip of the foil and epee is constructed in such a way that if the touch is too light, no signal is triggered.

The referee checks this with a weight before the bout begins.

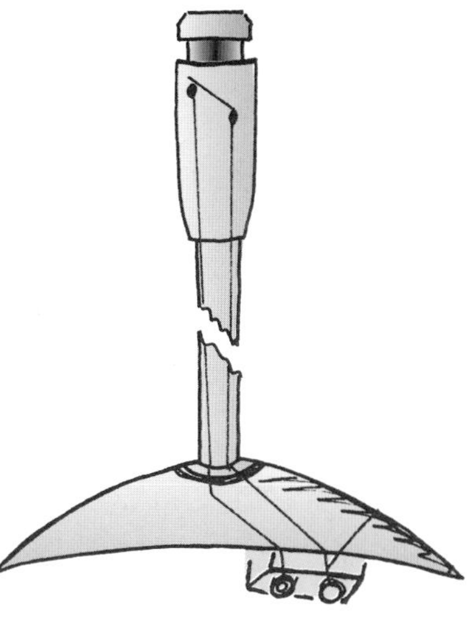

The tip of the foil must support a weight of **500 g** and the tip of the epee must support a weight of **750 g** without giving way.

Check your own weapon before a bout!

Electronical Equipment – Hooking Up the Fencer

Of course, your coach and your parents are happy to help you set up the technical equipment and don your gear. But isn't it more fun if you know how to do it yourself and don't always have to depend on others?

What a fencer needs

These are the equipment items that you must supply and keep in good working order:

- electronic weapon
- body cord
- for foil, metal vest
- for saber, special jacket, saber mask.

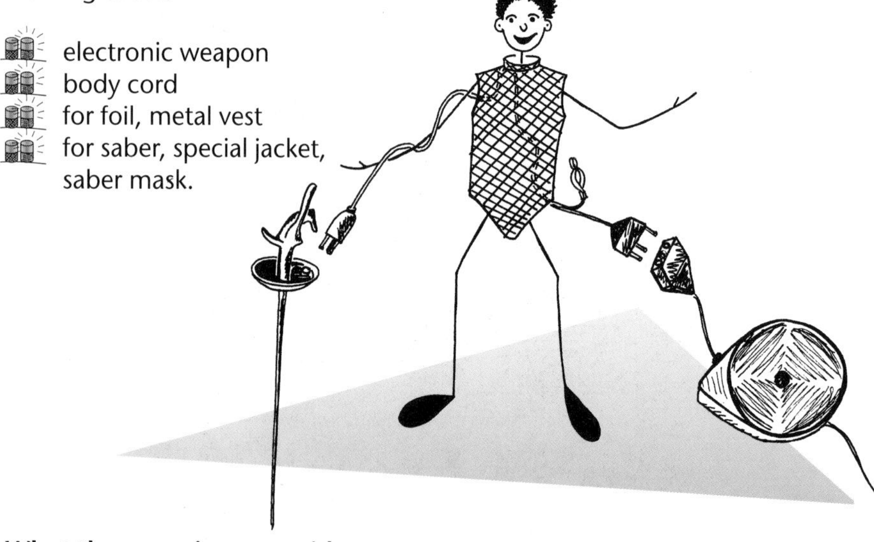

What the organizers provide

These are the equipment items that a tournament organizer provides. For practice sessions, of course, you are responsible for managing these:

- metal strip
- cable spool
- signal apparatus.

As in other areas of daily life, not everyone involved in fencing has the same degree of interest in the electronical equipment. Most fencers are happy if everything works, nothing goes wrong, or there's a technician around to fix a problem. Other fencers find it fascinating to take the equipment apart, put it back together, and figure out how it all works.

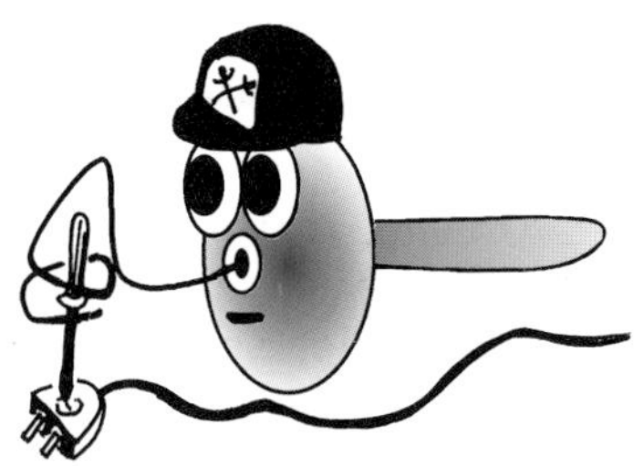

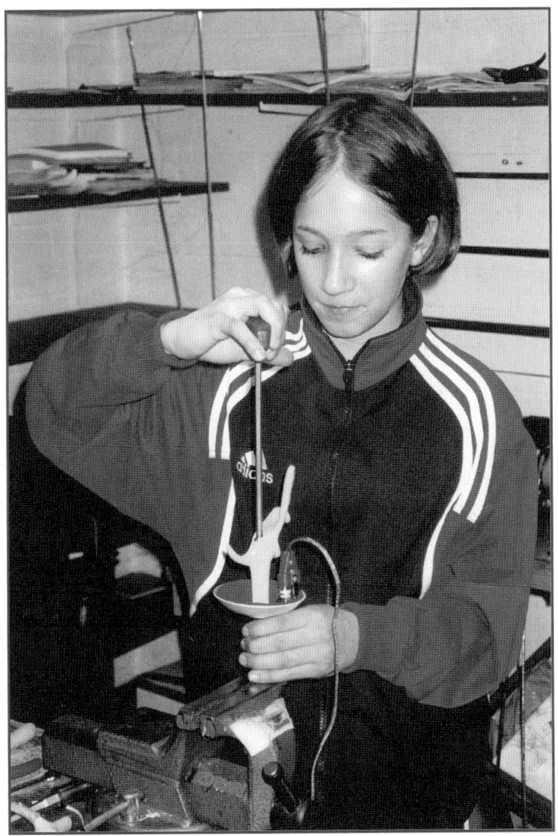

Don't Panic!

Whether you are interested in electronic equipment or not, you should have some technical understanding of the matter. You can check important aspects and fix minor malfunctions yourself. Then you won't always have to call for the coach or technician.

Here are the basic steps you need to know to solve common problems.

Problem: In foil or saber, the white light is always on. There's a break somewhere in the circuit.

- Inspect all the connections! Check that each plug is correctly and firmly inserted and that the clamps are fastened on the foil or saber.
- Release the connection between the body cord and the weapon. The white light is on. Bridge the two wires of the body cord with a screwdriver or the weapon guard. If the white light goes out, the weapon is defective and must be replaced.
- If the white light stays on, try substituting a different body cord. If the light goes out, the body cord must be replaced.
- If the white light stays on, the problem is in the cable roller, the floor cable, or the signal device.

Problem: In the test thrust with the foil, the white light goes on; or in the test stroke with the saber, no light goes on.

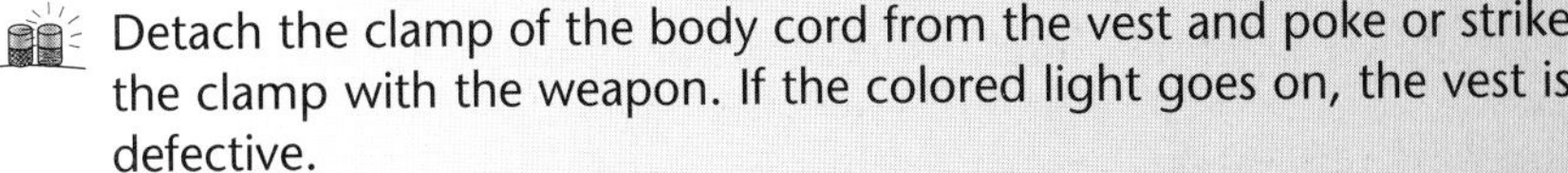

- Detach the clamp of the body cord from the vest and poke or strike the clamp with the weapon. If the colored light goes on, the vest is defective.
- If the colored light does not go on, check the body cord, the cable roller, or other connections.

Problem: In epee, the colored light does not go on when tested.

- Unplug the weapon and bridge the two prongs that are closer together with a screwdriver or the edge of the weapon guard. If the light goes on, the epee is defective.
- You can also test the body cord as described above.

If problems are intermittent, you can often identify the defective spot by wiggling the plugs, bending the blade, gently tapping the blade, or testing a loose tip.

Emergency tool kit

You don't need an entire tool chest in your fencing duffle, but it can be very helpful to have a few key items on hand.

Examples include:

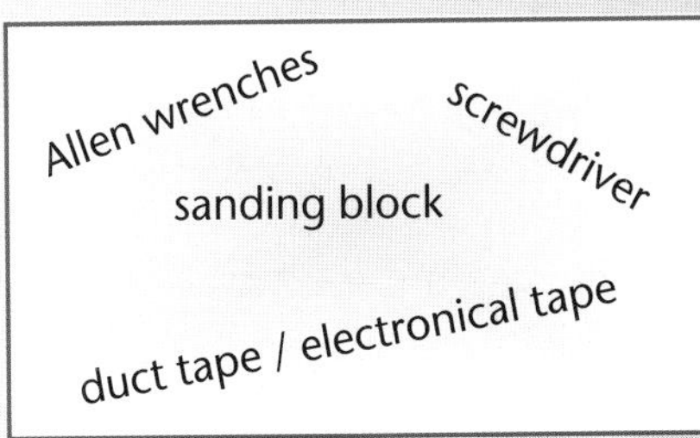

Allen wrenches
screwdriver
sanding block
duct tape / electronical tape

For Safe and Fair Competition

Inspect your fencing attire.

- A fencer enters the strip only in clean and functional fencing attire.

Inspect your mask.

- The wire mesh must be free of rust or other defects. Your safety is at stake.

Inspect your weapon.

- An old or defective blade could break off and badly injure an opponent.

Inspect your equipment before each competition.

- To keep the tournament running smoothly and avoid unnecessary delays, fencers should arrive with equipment inspected and in good working order. Keep replacement weapons and cables on hand for quick substitution.

The score is 4 : 4 in the bout. Max was behind, but he has pulled even. His opponent is nervous and unsure of himself. Max already has a good idea for his next action. He can pull it off!

But what's this? The white light goes on and stays on. Oh, no – not now, when everything is going so well!

The equipment is inspected; Max must replace his defective body cord. He had hoped that this old cord, with its wobbly plug, would make it through a few more bouts. If only he had checked it one more time! But yesterday, he had been too lazy to do it.

Now Max has all the stress of replacing his cord, while his opponent can take a few deep breaths and regain his concentration.

Who has the advantage when the bout resumes?

11 General Health

Anyone who thinks that hard, sweaty training several times a week is all that it takes to succeed in sports will soon learn otherwise. Sure, athletes must train if they are to progress, but they also need recovery periods, plenty of sleep, a healthy diet, good hygiene, a systematic training regimen, and much more.

You need to learn to recognize and listen to your body's "internal clock." Your body will tell you when you are in top form and when you urgently need to rest and relax. A good fencer also senses, for example, when he needs to eat high-energy food to help him concentrate and keep fencing well.

In this chapter, we have compiled some interesting information about staying in top form. We hope these ideas will encourage you to learn about your own body's performance, pay attention your "internal clock," and maintain a healthy diet.

Have fun!

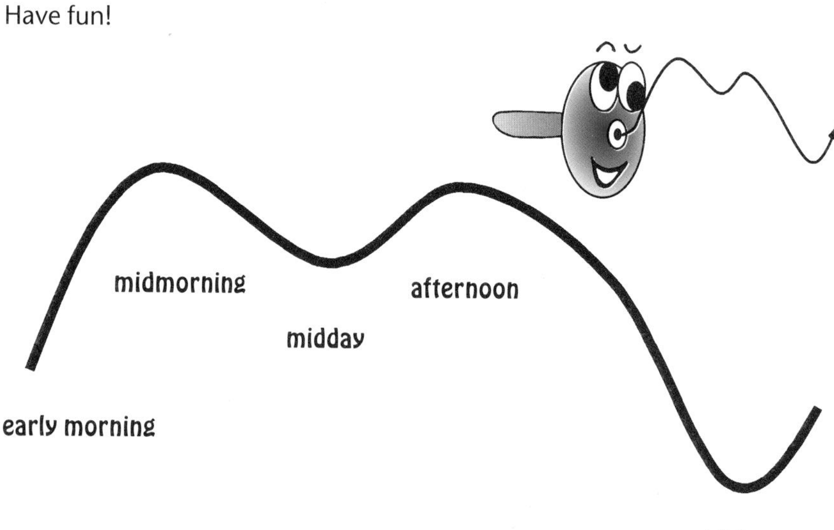

Our Ability to Perform

Over the course of a day, our ability to perform rises and falls, as you can see in the diagram above. The curve is similar for all human beings, and we have adjusted our lives accordingly. Most schools have lessons in the morning and afternoon, with a break for lunch (and probably a little free time). After school, perhaps it's time for playing outdoors, practicing sports, or engaging in other vigorous activity. At night, our bodies enjoy a well-earned rest. A person who follows this rhythm is more likely to stay healthy and fit. You can tell when you are working too hard or not getting enough sleep. Likewise, it would be a pity not to make good use of the peak performance hours.

Eat and Drink for Fitness!

Athletes who eat and drink too much before practice or competition, or eat and drink the wrong things, do not perform as well. They feel full and heavy; they look tired and listless. Many bodily functions slow down when the stomach is in high gear. But we must eat to supply our bodies with the energy we need; even more important, we must drink to make up for the fluid we lose when we perspire. We also need to eat and drink during longer training sessions and competitions.

The following table can help you determine what you should or should not eat and drink at meals, at snack time, and in between for an extra boost of energy. Choose your food and beverages and time your intake so that you have plenty of energy for training and competitions, but your body does not also have to work to digest food during these sessions.

How long food stays in the stomach before it is digested:

About 1 hour:	water, tea, clear soups
About 2–3 hours:	cocoa, bananas, apples, dinner rolls, rice, cooked fish, soft-cooked eggs, whole-grain bread, cake, bread and butter, granola, vegetables
About 4–5 hours:	sausages, meat, baked potatoes, French fries, beans or peas
About 6–7 hours:	rich cake, mushrooms, fried fish, fatty meats.

The food pyramid shows which foods you should enjoy plentifully and which you should eat only sparingly. A few examples are listed for each food group.

The Food Pyramid

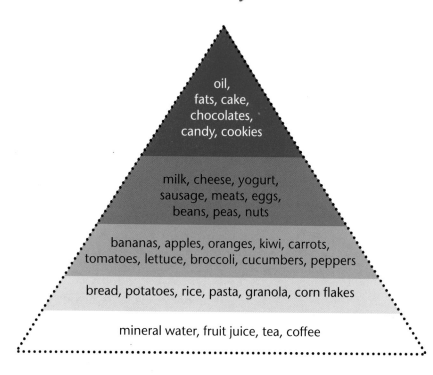

oil,
fats, cake,
chocolates,
candy, cookies

milk, cheese, yogurt,
sausage, meats, eggs,
beans, peas, nuts

bananas, apples, oranges, kiwi, carrots,
tomatoes, lettuce, broccoli, cucumbers, peppers

bread, potatoes, rice, pasta, granola, corn flakes

mineral water, fruit juice, tea, coffee

Sources of Energy

You can achieve peak physical performance only if you provide your body with enough energy (sugar and starch) in the form of food.

If you take in just the right amount, you will perform at your best. If you take in too little, your performance and concentration will suffer, and you will feel tired. On the other hand, if you supply your body with too much energy, you run the risk of becoming jittery and getting tired more quickly.

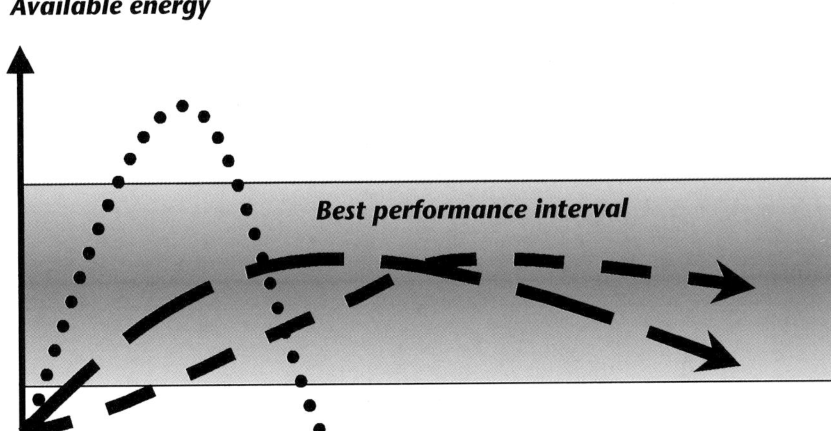

Sweets, honey, glucose, sweetened drinks give you quick energy and a sudden boost in performance. But this does not last long.

Milk drinks, candy bars fortified with milk, and apples give you quick energy that remains available for a longer time.

Granola, whole-grain products, and bananas do not give you a sudden boost of energy, but the energy they provide is available for a longer time.

If You Sweat, Drink Plenty of Fluids

Athletes need to drink copiously to replenish the fluids they lose by sweating during training sessions and competitions. Otherwise, your performance suffers. Your blood becomes thicker; it can carry less oxygen, and your muscles will cramp.

Suitable drinks before and during exercise
Mineral water, fruit juice mixed with seltzer in a ratio of about 1:3, lightly sweetened beverages.

Suitable drinks after exercise
Fruit juice mixed with less seltzer, milk-based drinks, beverages with a higher sugar content.

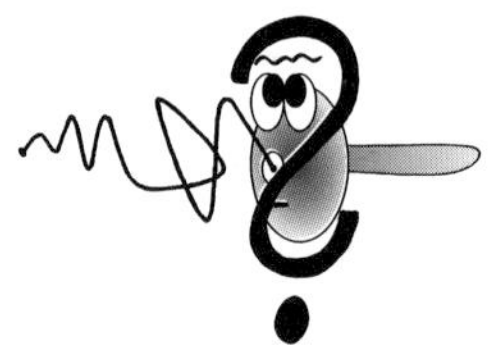

Can you find 16 fruits and vegetables listed horizontally, vertically, or diagonally?

M	K	A	P	O	T	A	T	O	E	S	A	B	I	F
Z	U	C	C	H	I	N	I	D	N	J	R	Q	U	A
K	N	U	I	S	E	G	N	A	R	O	T	T	B	A
I	S	C	A	L	E	T	T	U	C	E	I	A	L	H
S	Q	U	A	S	H	O	K	C	G	R	A	P	E	S
K	A	M	T	H	L	E	O	E	R	N	Q	W	M	E
S	K	B	Y	E	J	L	A	S	A	O	N	P	O	H
G	H	E	R	P	I	N	E	A	P	P	L	E	N	C
C	A	R	R	O	T	S	J	O	E	H	N	P	S	A
V	E	S	R	M	P	O	N	T	F	S	R	P	P	N
S	E	I	R	R	E	B	W	A	R	T	S	E	X	I
S	A	N	A	N	A	B	C	E	U	L	I	R	A	P
L	C	L	I	Z	R	A	I	M	I	R	N	S	E	S
X	C	M	F	L	S	J	V	S	T	A	R	K	Z	J

Rebus: What Is This?

Do you know the feeling of getting out of bed the day after a training session and feeling stiff and sore all over? Every step is painful. Your arms hurt when you brush your teeth, and walking down stairs makes your thighs ache. And oh, dear, if someone tells a joke and you can't help laughing...how your abdominal muscles complain! When you tell your coach about it, he answers: "You have stiff muscles."

When do stiff muscles happen?

If you work your muscles especially hard or in new and different ways, you can get stiff and sore. The muscles simply aren't used to the effort. The probability of sore muscles is higher when you practice new exercises, resume training after a long pause, or train especially hard. Beginners aren't the only ones who get stiff and sore; even top-flight athletes feel the effects of unaccustomed effort.

What are stiff muscles, anyway?

To put it quite simply, if you haven't ever moved in a certain way, or if you haven't done so for a long time, your muscles don't really know what to do. They lack the coordination to work smoothly. As a result, tiny injuries occur within the muscle. The cells release substances that cause pain, and the muscles become tense and tight.

It was once thought that the pain was caused by lactic acid that accumulated in the cells after sustained physical exertion. We now know that this is not the case. The small tears in the muscle tissue are what hurt.

Why do I get stiff muscles the day after I train hard?

It isn't the unaccustomed movements that cause soreness, but the fluid released into the muscles because of the mini-injuries. That doesn't happen right away; you generally don't feel it until the next day. Unfortunately, it also takes a day or two for the pain to go away.

What's wrong with you?

Oh, coach, I'm stiff as a board!

What should I do for stiff muscles?

It's easy to get stiff muscles, harder to get rid of them! It takes time for the muscles to repair themselves. A stressed muscle needs rest and care so the tiny tears in the muscle tissue can heal. Heat is beneficial; take a warm bath or a sauna. Massages or infrared treatment can also help.

You can also take active steps to ease your sore muscles. Try gentle relaxation exercises or the stretches we described earlier. Just be sure not to stretch so much that it hurts.

Can I go to practice if I have stiff muscles?

Of course you can continue your training sessions. Protect the sore muscles and concentrate on other movements for a while. For example, if your legs are stiff, you can spend more time doing arm exercises with the target dummy, or practice parries with a partner.

Is there a way to prevent stiff muscles?

Muscle injuries, even small ones, are more likely when cold muscles are put to work. Don't forget to warm up and stretch! Also, start with a slow and gentle effort, and then increase the level of exertion. You can't walk into the fencing hall and do ten lunges right off the bat! If you haven't been able to train for a while, start slowly and don't overdo it. The best way to prevent soreness is to train regularly and keep your muscles toned.

Stiff muscles aren't an illness!

12 Fair Play

Sports are fun, and winning at competitive sports is even more fun. But imagine that you could do anything and everything to defeat your opponent...

What if you could add a special button to your weapon so that you could make the light go on whenever you liked? What if you could smear glue on the soles of your opponent's shoes? What if you could bribe the referee so he would favor you, or take drugs so you would never get out of breath? How much fun would winning be then?

Now what's the matter?

Boohoo! Coach, that was so unfair! My opponent kept pretending to thrust. When I was just about to parry, he disengaged and scored a point!

That wasn't unfair – that was a feint. The rules allow feinting. You should try it yourself sometime!

Furthermore, what does any of that have to do with fencing, technique, or tactics? Nothing, of course! Like all other sports, fencing has rules that specify which behaviors and materials are allowed and how actions and touches are judged. Fencers who fail to abide by these conventions are warned or even banned from competition.

Within the rules, you can do everything in your power to win. That includes speed in your steps, lunges, and parries; it also includes good tactics. You study your opponent, maneuver him into a position that's favorable to you, surprise him by sudden movements, and trick him by feinting. You rely on your experience from other bouts, and you carry yourself with a confident air. You can make use of all the fencing skills you have learned in your training sessions and all the skills we have described in this book.

My Athletic Opponent – Not My Enemy

You can sing by yourself, or dance, run, and swim. But to fence properly, you need a partner. When we speak of the opponent in fencing, we are describing a partner who challenges us to do our best, a partner who tests our fencing skills, a partner whom we try hard to defeat in a bout. Without an opponent, fencing is no fun at all. Therefore, it makes sense to treat this opponent with courtesy and respect. Strive to be honorable and friendly. Gracefully acknowledge a better performance.

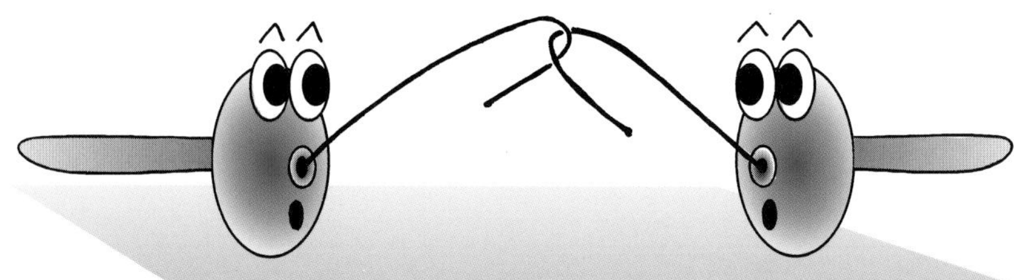

Paul and Max are best friends. They started fencing together as beginners. Recently, Paul has been losing almost every bout, and naturally he's rather depressed about it. He has even thought of giving up fencing.

In the next bout between the two friends, Max deliberately holds back so that Paul will win. Paul is elated! Later, the coach takes Max aside and asks him why he let Paul win. Max is astonished at the question; after all, even the coach has noticed how unhappy Paul was.

Max tells the coach, "But you told us yourself that we were supposed to be fair to each other!"

What do you think about Max's behavior? He's a real pal, right? Or maybe not. Perhaps in this instance he didn't completely understand the idea of "playing fair."

Can you help the coach think of other ways that Max could be a true friend to Paul?

....

....

....

....

....

....

The Sportsmanship Award for Willi Kothny

When two friends train in the same club, they often practice partner exercises together or coach each other. They help each other, give each other tips, and have fun in their training bouts. But sometimes this friendship is also put to a hard test. The test is called competition! When the two friends meet in a tournament, the time for helping each other is over. Each does her best, because only one can win.

The German saber fencers Willi Kothny and Ero Lehmann are friends who trained together for the 2000 Olympic Games in Sydney. They met in the Olympic tournament. Ero lost and was eliminated. Of course, he was not happy about it, but he congratulated Willi, quickly changed out of his fencing attire, and cheered Willy on in his next bouts. Willi went on to win the bronze medal in singles.

Because Ero had lost so early in the singles, for the team competition his coach selected him as just a substitute. This saber team also won the bronze. Now Willi Kothny had two Olympic medals. Unfortunately, there are no medals for substitutes at the Olympics. At the awards ceremony, Willi handed his bronze medal to Ero. Not in jest, as Ero might have thought, but for keeps!

When asked why he had done this, Willi (whose name is actually Wiradech) answered,

"Simple! It's nice to win, but it's also nice to have a good friend."

For this gesture, the ARD broadcasting network awarded Wiradech Kothny its sportsmanship award, the **Victoria**.

What is fair and what is unfair in a fencing match? After you decide, draw an arrow to the side you chose.

salute before
the bout

yelling at the referee
because he made
the wrong call

bribing the referee

feinting

studying your opponent
during a bout

doping

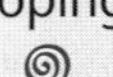

making fun of
your opponent

distance game

feint

modifying your weapon
so a touch
is scored sooner

pretending to be weak
on defense

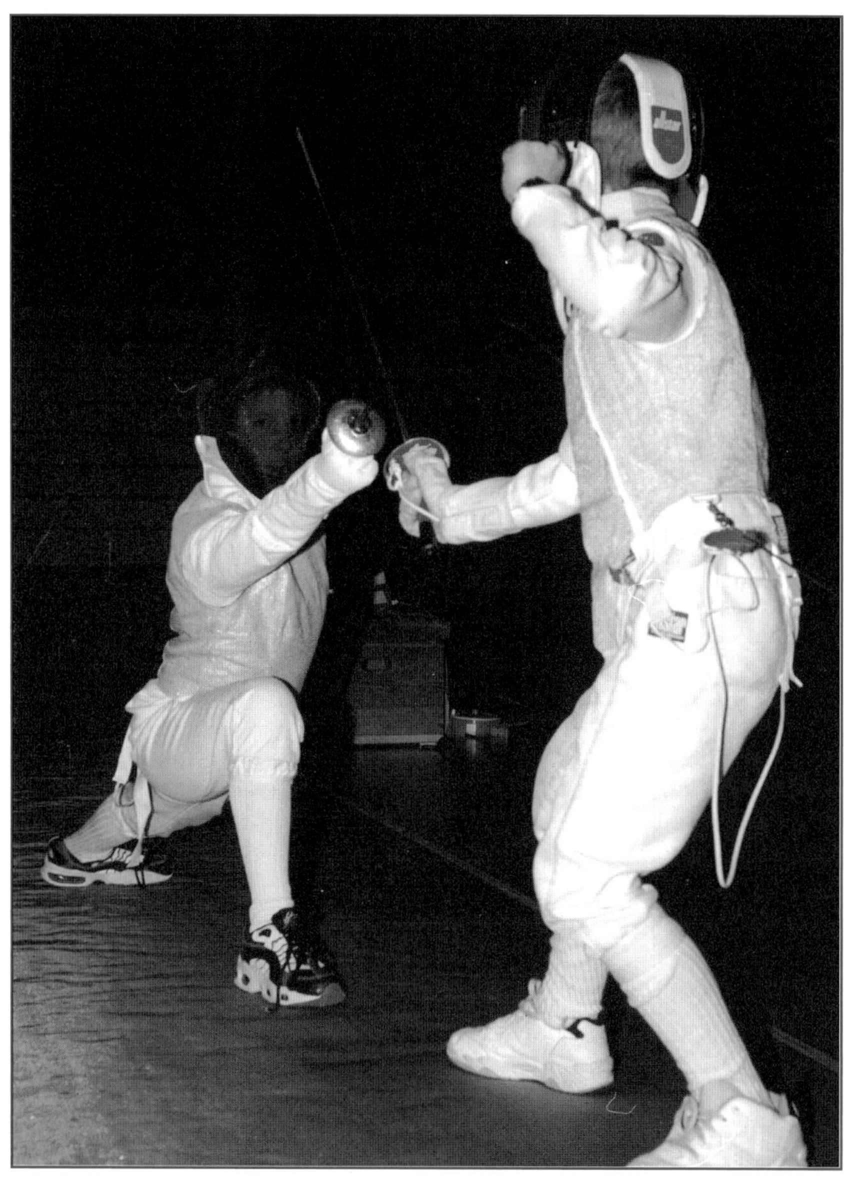

13 Answers and Solutions

Page 36 Of course, Paul is smarter, precisely because he has to work harder. As a result, his muscles will get stronger. Pia thinks she is getting away with something, but she's only hurting herself, because when she exercises without effort, her performance won't improve.

Page 44 Weightlifting, for example.
Page 45 Distance running, for example.
Page 46 Sprinting, for example.
Page 46 Fencing, for example.

Page 65

KAONGDFU**CONTACT**LENG**FEINT**LOEBNKKGJJDITTMER
KPUWMV**JUMP**OSPRULEFV**PARRY**SLPQMO**PRIORITY**FJOS
FLECHESHBIR**RETREAT**AKLE**LUNGE**WUOLQWDAFBSER
NVAMCUSHJAFGA**BEAT**MNASSIO**ADVANCE**DKLCCBOHA
TWBXKABUNOSLI**OCTAVE**LOUVSTOA**THRUST**GBAJOHRB

Page 74 This is not really a punishment, because the extra time she spends with the coach will improve Sally's skills. It would actually be more appropriate to give the extra coaching to the fencers who have worked especially hard in practice.

Page 95 D,B,A,C

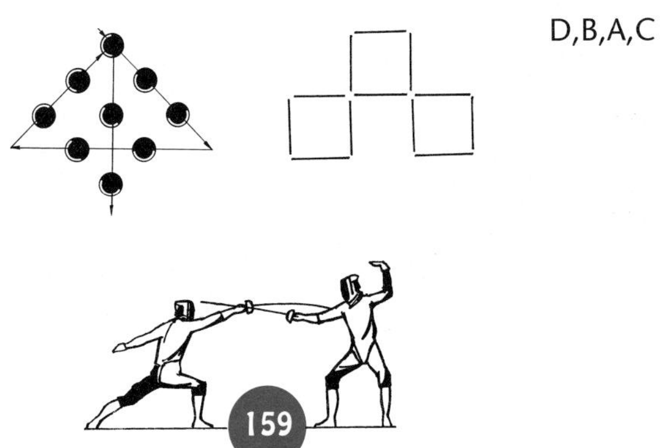

Pages 96–97 Test

12–15 points

With your attitude toward sports, you could go far. You enjoy competition, and you have good sportsmanship and self-discipline. Keep it up!

8–11 points

You have a good attitude toward sports, but sometimes you don't try as hard as you could. If you took more pleasure in the effort and were more competitive, you might be more successful as a fencer.

5–7 points

If all you think about is yourself, fencing is not the right sport for you. You need to work on your attitude in regard to fairness and team spirit. Take your training and competition seriously, treat other athletes with respect, and enjoy fencing.

Page 111 The beetle does **not** reach his sweetheart.

Page 148

M	K	A	P	O	T	A	T	O	E	S	A	B	I	F
Z	U	C	C	H	I	N	I	D	N	J	R	Q	U	A
K	N	U	I	S	E	G	N	A	R	O	T	T	B	A
I	S	C	A	L	E	T	T	U	C	E	I	A	L	H
S	Q	U	A	S	H	O	K	C	G	R	A	P	E	S
K	A	M	T	H	L	E	O	E	R	N	Q	W	M	E
S	K	B	Y	E	J	L	A	S	A	O	N	P	O	H
G	H	E	R	P	I	N	E	A	P	P	L	E	N	C
C	A	R	R	O	T	S	J	O	E	H	N	P	S	A
V	E	S	R	M	P	O	N	T	F	S	R	P	P	N
S	E	I	R	R	E	B	W	A	R	T	S	E	X	I
S	A	N	A	N	A	B	C	E	U	L	I	R	A	P
L	C	L	I	Z	R	A	I	M	I	R	N	S	E	S
X	C	M	F	L	S	J	V	S	T	A	R	K	Z	J

14 A Message to Parents and Coaches

Dear Parents:

Your child enjoys fencing! Otherwise, he would have stopped his lessons, rather than signing up for more. It's important for you to know why he is continuing with training. Talk with your child about it, or ask him to show you the pages in this book about his motives.

You can assume one thing, however: A person who trains for fencing wants to succeed and likes to win. Those who take up fencing in the first place have at least a tendency to be fighters and winners. Those who continue training in earnest will foster and cultivate these characteristics – qualities that can be very useful in other areas of life as well. We have found that training for fencing has positive effects on overall health and personality development.

The theories, experience, and knowledge of how to train young fencers, working systematically to achieve goals over the long term, are many and varied. The optimal course of training recommended by the Deutscher Fechter-Bund in its overall training program is shown in the overview below. You will be interested to know the stages at which certain abilities or qualities should be developed, to what degree, and how they should be evaluated in order to determine the next appropriate training tasks.

At various points in this book, we give pointers that young fencers can follow to check and assess their own progress. Share in these activities; help your child, and show her that you are interested in her progress.

Basic Training, 11–12 years old

Goals, primary skills, training methods:

- Diversified overall training of motor skills, oriented toward speed and mobility.
- Varied technical training (emphasizing speed and rhythm) and introduction to tactics.
- Development of independence and long-term motivation for fencing.
- Introduction to training with a partner.
- Ratio of general and specialized training is about 50:50.

Advanced Training, 13–14 years old

Goals, primary skills, training methods:

- Solidify a varied repertoire of techniques and tactics while increasing speed and reactions.
- Identify particular strengths and begin to develop specific strengths through lessons.
- Competition has two functions: it is both a complex form of training and a demonstration of skill.
- Begin training oriented toward winning and behavior.
- Ratio of general and specialized training is about 30:70.

The ages given here are approximate, of course. A child who takes up fencing at age 12 will start advanced training somewhat later.

This book about training for fencing was written for young fencers. Our goal is to help them better understand their sport. We offer advice about how to train properly.

We hope children and young people will learn to recognize their own potential and be more aware of how to work with their own bodies. This will not only promote more effective training, but also prevent possible under- or over-training. With a sound basis of knowledge, we can challenge our children appropriately as they develop.

Dear Coach:

Effective training for young athletes takes into consideration the overall personality development of children and youth. As a learning activity, athletic training both relies on guidance and promotes self-control. Training has a socializing effect; group training, in particular, brings to bear societal norms, rules, and behavior patterns. Training for children and youth is experiential. Respecting moods, sensitivities, and feelings, effective training ensures positive experiences, develops needs and desires, and takes place in a cordial, loving, and open atmosphere.

As a coach, you can't achieve these goals on your own. You need the fencers. They are your partners – provided that you actively include them, while giving them the freedom to meet their own needs. Children and adolescents are very willing and able to adapt. The youthful drive toward independence and self-awareness is seemingly unlimited.

By now, you will have asked how you can make the most of this potential. Quite simply: View your young fencers not as clay to be molded, but as partners in a shared enterprise. Tell them when and why a certain exercise is necessary, and why they should work hard on a particular aspect of their training program, at a particular time.

You may ask whether such specificity is even possible – and of course, it is not. True, there is a widespread demand for age-appropriate sequences of exercises, training, and exertion that take into consideration general models of biological, psychological, and pedagogical stages of development. Such training programs, based on very generalized average data, offer a rough framework of orientation for estimating the developmental status of individual children and adolescents.

What a young athlete needs, however, are challenges appropriate to his or her particular biological stage of development and training history. You will encounter early, normal and late developers, as well as novices and experienced athletes. A young person's calendar age alone does not tell you all you need to know. In this age group, the biological age can vary by two to three years on either side of the calendar age. That is, a 12-year-old child may have the body of an average 10-year-old (late developer) or a typical 14-year-old (early developer). The biologically younger child must be given time to develop, and you must not expect too much of the biologically older child. Each child is different.

As a coach, your task is to fine-tune a general training program to suit the athletes under your supervision, presenting challenges at just the right level for each young fencer. Effective coaching calls for a skillful combination and interplay of pedagogical guidance and independence.

This training book will help you in this endeavor. You know how much time you can spend simply explaining various aspects of fencing to your young charges. We have expertly compiled that essential information here in an easily understandable form, so that each child can read it over at home. Particularly if your club can offer practice sessions only once or twice a week, you must rely on your young fencers to train on their own as well if they are to keep pace with others. Then, too, you surely want to use your precious time in the fencing hall for active training, not for lectures and explanations. We invite you to use this book the way a schoolteacher uses a textbook or a piano instructor uses a practice book. The modern concept of "active training" calls for independent goal setting, self-motivation, self-monitoring, and self-evaluation. An important developmental goal in training young athletes is that they learn to determine their own level of expectations and to carefully increase the difficulty of the tasks they set themselves. But to accomplish this, they need information and understanding. This book provides that.

Young fencers are living, growing creatures, not merely passive objects of our influence. They need room to develop their potential. Sometimes we fail to encourage independence in our young fencers – independence that, rightly used, would enhance the intensity and above all the quality of a training program. Effective coaches of young athletes never forget that their task involves more than teaching fencing techniques and building fitness. Coaches who engage young fencers in their own training not only improve the overall quality of the training sessions, but also consciously foster the development of the athlete as a whole person.

We assume that fencers can and should take increasing responsibility for their own personal development as part of the learning process. As they do so, training sessions can focus more and more on technical and tactical training. However, coaches must systematically help their young athletes work toward this goal.

We, the authors, wish you continued pleasure and success with your fencers!

Photo & Illustration Credits

Cover photo:	Sportpressefoto Bongarts, Hamburg
Graphics:	Katrin Barth
Photos:	Jochen Färber, FC Tauberbischofsheim, Wiratech Kothny, Dr. Hans M. Rupp, Ingo Staffehl, Bodo Stutzke
Cover design:	Birgit Engelen, Stolberg

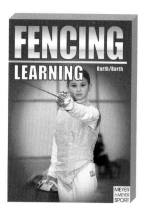